1981

NURSING

FINANCE

Budgeting Strategies
for a New Age

by

Tim Porter-O'Grady, R.N., Ed.D., CNAA
Senior Health Consultant
Master Consultants, Inc.
Atlanta, GA

Coordinator of Mercy Mobile
Health Project
Atlanta, GA

AN ASPEN PUBLICATION®
Aspen Publishers, Inc.

1987

Rockville, Maryland
Royal Tunbridge Wells

Library of Congress Cataloging-in-Publication Data

Porter-O'Grady, Timothy.
Nursing finance.

Includes index.
1. Nursing services—Business management. 2. Budget.
I. Title. [DNLM: 1. Administrative Personnel.
2. Financial Management—methods—nurses' instruction.
WY 77 P847n]   RT86.7.P67   1987   362.1'   73'0681
ISBN: 0-87189-856-X

Editorial Services: Lisa J. McCullough
Mary Beth Roesser

Library of Congress Catalog Card Number: 87-14546
ISBN: 0-87189-856-X

Printed in the United States of America

1   2   3   4   5

To Tom and Mardie, my parents:
After many years, my grateful thanks.

Table of Contents

Special Note

In keeping with my established pattern in texts of this kind, the pronoun reference to "she" is used throughout this book. While I recognize that many men are nurses and will be using this text, the preponderance of readers will be women nurses. The use of "she" recognizes this reality. However, it is not intended to ignore the fact that there are men in the profession and that they make many fine contributions to nursing. "She" is used simply to maintain consistency and to recognize the gender realities of nursing.

Preface

As the world of health care changes, so also will all the processes associated with managing its affairs. As a result of this reality, many of the systems and approaches used to manage health care services will be altered in a radical way, leaving the manager with the need for new tools and resources to help her sort through the maze of new processes and procedures that represent the demand for unique approaches to health care management.

Since 1981, a major transition in structure, focus, and process in the delivery of health care services has occurred. With the introduction of the prospective payment system, much of this transition has been orientated to establishing a more businesslike framework for the delivery of services. New terminology such as diagnosis related groups, market share, health care products, and product line management have been introduced, bringing with them a need for a new set of skills and resources necessary for success in the new marketplace.

The historic reality of good management, however, does not change. Any manager can learn the skills and techniques essential to success. She need only have the right tools in order to excel in the role. This book presents some basic tools involving the newer concepts of health care delivery having an impact on financial management.

Good resource management is an even greater necessity for the nurse manager of today and tomorrow than traditionally has been expected. The operation of a nursing unit, department, or service now parallels the function of any other business unit in other kinds of services. Applying the concept of service orientation and business strategies to the management of human and fiscal resources, the nurse executive can be assured of having the skills necessary to do the planning and managing well into the 21st century. The framework within which such skills are applied, however, changes continually. It is these changes that must be addressed by good managers and sound financial planners.

Consistent with the role of planner is the ability to develop and generate data that can serve as an informational base to assist the manager in making decisions regarding the viability of her financial plan and the success of her service operations. The successful manager will be able judiciously to juggle the roles of data gatherer, interpreter, and decisionmaker during this difficult transitional period and beyond. The nurse leader on the front lines of management must take advantage of the opportunity to develop the skills needed to direct the business of nursing care services regardless of what they might be. Developing the conceptual base and the financial planning framework with all the constituent pieces—creativity, strategic planning, forecasting, assessment, fiscal control, and resource evaluation—will support the manager in providing effective leadership into the next several decades.

It is not the purpose of this text to provide the full range of information the manager needs in order to operate successfully within the new financial framework. Rather, it is designed to be one of a number of references that the nursing leader will have in her armamentarium of information and tools as she develops skills as a fiscal manager. The author does not pretend that this is a complete representation of the full range of financial processes having an impact on the role of the manager. What it is designed to accomplish is to introduce the front-line manager to the concepts and processes of financial planning, budgeting, and control. Utilizing this text as one of a number of resources is the best possible way to obtain value from it. It also should serve as one tool for developing the nursing corporate division or corporate system managers to assume responsibility and to acquire skills for fiscal management of clinical services.

As always, there are more challenges ahead than those of the past. This book, in association with other suggested readings, can help the nurse manager meet these new challenges, provide leadership in health care services, and guide their future direction. The nurse manager's ability to do all that successfully is predicated on her strong commitment to her own development and growth in both applying and sharing a variety of systematic approaches to finance and services. Her peers and the nursing staff will look to her for leadership in moving boldly into the 21st century.

Tim Porter-O'Grady

Acknowledgments

The preparation of a manuscript such as this is rarely the product of any one individual. Many persons have helped in numerous and detailed ways in giving form to this book. My thanks to Mark Ponder, colleague and friend, for his inspiration, insight, and support; Sharon Finnigan, partner and friend, who has been with me in good times and bad; Carol Kobler, for her participation in the preparation of this book; my nursing colleagues, who always serve as sources of inspiration and renewal as together we look to lead health care into the 21st century; and finally, those who continue to share their love and support in my personal growth: as always, I am blessed and grateful.

Planning: The Cornerstone of Nursing Finance

OBJECTIVES FOR CHAPTER 1

This chapter will:
1. *Discuss the components of a clearly outlined planning process for financial budgeting.*
2. *Outline the relationship between performance and outcomes and their dependencies on accurate performance standards.*
3. *Clarify the objective planning process as a tool for defining budget and finance goals.*
4. *Provide specific tools for developing an organized and systematic approach to goal setting.*
5. *Identify specific services and personnel supportive to the nurse manager in the development of this financial planning process.*

It should come as no surprise that the health care business is in a new age of finance. Ever since the introduction of the prospective payment system (PPS) in 1983, there have been radical changes in the health care delivery system. Major components of those changes are directed to the financing of health care services. While it is not the intent to detail here the PPS components and their impact, much of this book reflects a response to it.

Because of these many new demands, nurses in management are required to develop knowledge and a skill base in overseeing the nursing division's finances. This has been an onerous task for most nurses, and appears to be getting more so every day. The demands on nurse managers in both time and in developing competence in finance seem to be growing as a percentage of the time they spend in management activities. They often feel that much of what is happening is beyond their understanding and often is not within their mindset. After all, most nurses

have been educated for clinical practice and have evolved to the role of manager
without much preparation for such a role. It is quite a shock to be thrust suddenly
into the world of facts, figures, and dollars without substantial preparation in what
they are and how to manage them.

The problem is that these new managers generally lack appropriate tools and
supports. Much of the literature, while helpful, is beyond the grasp of those not
prepared in a financial specialty. Even the language of finance seems a foreign
tongue. The processes often are difficult to grasp and some of the rules seem to
change from year to year. Just when the manager feels she has the system under
control, it changes in the next budget year, largely in response to changes in tax
laws or in governmental constraints seeking to contain health care costs. The manager feels as though she operates at the mercy of the system and never can work
herself out of its grip.

Perhaps the best defense in such a case is a good offense. True, much of finance
can be confusing. The nurse manager's task, therefore, is not to lament its va-
garies but to learn as much as possible about the financial process, then put it to
use for her needs. It is to this purpose that this book is committed. The financial
process is unfolded step by step in an elemental manner, not because it must be
kept simple but because this is the best way to develop an integrated view of the
process and all of its parts. The goal is to paint a picture of the nursing operation
so that managers can get a sense of how it looks and its characteristics that will
affect their success.

It is best to begin by saying simply that all that finance amounts to is the creation of a numeric picture of what nurse managers are about—that provides a detailed analysis of what they are doing and where it will lead them and their service.
Finance, for the nurse manager, will always reflect the reality of her goals, operations, and outcomes. Since nursing operates in a social enterprise that is driven
by the economy, the number of dollars available will determine the kind and quality of activities that can be undertaken.

It is a truism that when one has more, one can do more. The manager of the
department, service, or unit must get all she can out of the resources available,
or risk losing the job. This is one of the guiding principles of the financial process
in today's economic system. This book, as noted, is focused on acquainting the
manager with the mechanics of the process as it applies to nursing in the hope
that such understanding will position her better to function and to make changes
and improvements.

CREATING A GOOD FINANCIAL PLAN

The starting point in any good financial picture is the plan it represents. Skills
in the financial planning process are essential for good management. The com-

mitment to planning must exist at every level of the organization. The nursing divisional and unit plans must reflect this process. Integration of nursing into the institution's goals and its other constituent parts is vital if the financial plan is to operate effectively.

Planning begins with some sense of where the institution is going. The grand design must address issues of mission, purposes, and direction. The processes for undertaking this mission need to be identified by the highest levels of the institution, usually at the board level. The plan should be disseminated to all levels of the organization that will share some responsibility for making it work. There should be no secrets. The issue of "confidentiality" in the purpose and direction of the organization has caused many unnecessary problems in many health care facilities. Holding back meaningful information at the planning level creates two conditions, both of them disastrous: (1) It provides inadequate information for doing the job effectively and (2) It leads to a high level of mistrust. Organizations that operate in such a manner pay a high price for it. They will have more problems than they can handle in confronting their economic viability over the long haul.

There are basic rules to successful financial planning. Once learned and practiced, they can serve the manager effectively.

Simplicity

The simpler the plan, the clearer it will be. Long, detailed, convoluted planning statements should be avoided. Anything worth accomplishing is worth understanding. The plan should be straightforward and simply written. It generally can be expressed in one sentence. Simple plans have a much better chance of being evaluated accurately.

"Snowjob" or grandiose and wordy planning statements don't do anyone any good. They are a waste of time and fail to accomplish anything. If the planning process is a matter of rote and is undertaken simply because it reflects the organization's expectations, then there clearly are problems with management's investment in the viability and future of the institution. "Keep it simple, keep it clear" is the best rule to follow in developing the plan.

Goals and Directions

The goals and directions of the department or unit must be consistent with and reflect the overall objectives of the institution. It is pointless to develop divisional plans that in some way do not mesh with the institution's own plans. Departments may have wonderful ideas for offering services and expanding their service base, or the institution's, that may respond well to the marketplace yet not truly reflect the facility's mission and goals.

If the plan is viable and can indeed influence the institution positively, that should be indicated in its mission or purpose. The relationship here is very important because if there is a failure of integration in the planning phase, there is a strong possibility there will be trouble in the operational phase. Pulling together at planning time will set the course for sound operating behavior.

Supporting Data

The department or unit nurse manager must collect supporting data to make sure that the direction sought is viable. Many times goals are based on feelings and conjecture, neither of which should be the sole basis for making decisions. Demographic, geographic, and statistical data reflecting the marketability of the goal are important supports in designing the program. These hard data back up what the manager feels might be a viable and appropriate direction to take with a program or service. Such justification adds considerable strength to her efforts in getting her division's or unit's goals accepted.

Assessment of the Competition

This is both an internal and an external requirement. Many goals vie for approval inside the institution; each one is important and presumably can advance the facility's purposes. Nursing goals will compete with other departments or units for the resources available. Not all will be approved. A good manager determines as fairly and fully as possible what kind of program competition exists. The nurse manager's program can be strengthened further where there is an opportunity to share resources with others whose goals are compatible or to support another service through the achievement of her own goals.

External competition provides a different type of influence to contend with. In the new payment system, head-on competition with the same mix of services as competing institutions provide no longer may be the best strategy if only for the reason that the population available to utilize those offerings may be limited. In such circumstances, the nurse manager may be competing for a limited population, and dividing it with other institutions may reduce her long-term possibilities and profitability. The facility's marketing department should make a careful assessment of the service market and the institution's relationship to it; this is an essential first step in the nursing division's own planning process. Care and caution must be taken at the earliest stages of the planning process so that expensive resources are not committed precipitously.

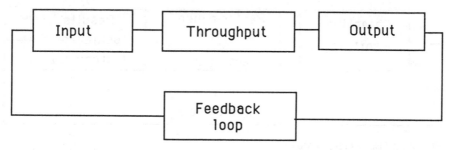

Figure 1-1 Communication Process Model

The Communication Process

The planning process is a systematic and basic corollary to the financial process. A cybernetic approach is one that often is recommended as a conceptual guide to the planning and communication process.

A communication process model (Figure 1-1) is appropriate here because a planning document essentially is a communication tool. Each of the elements of the cybernetic pathway should be addressed in any plan that seeks to communicate the action that will be taken in any given period. The manager then assures that her planning document is complete and has addressed all the issues of concern to those who must approve and implement its recommendations.

The process of putting the cybernetic process into practical use simply means developing a format for the planning process that should result in a complete and meaningful program. The planning process components thus must be clearly structured so that the same results can always be anticipated. The ability to structure a plan containing the elements and information required to communicate accurately what is to be accomplished is central to successful unfolding of a viable program to which the institution can commit resources for its completion.

The operational model in Figure 1-2 provides a reasonable framework for such a plan. It utilizes the components of objective, performance standard, time values, and outcomes expected and achieved. While there are variations on this theme, this is an effective framework for any planning process at the departmental or unit level.

Writing Objectives

The writing of objectives can be both simple and complex. The complexity relates to the manager's attempt to keep the objectives simple yet to address clearly the activity that must be described. Presenting objectives in terms of expected outcomes is essential in structuring them—after all, the manager is inter-

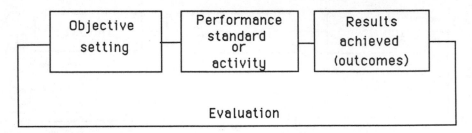

Figure 1-2 Planning Process Model

ested in achieving something. A succinct statement of what that something is is the best format for objective writing.

A good guide to keep in mind in writing such a statement is to relate the objective to the completion of an event or a time frame. For example:

"Upon the completion of this program . . . "

"By the end of the first quarter . . . "

"At the end of this project . . . "

"By June 1, 199_ . . . "

Following the lead-in statement, the desired outcome should be stated. The lead-in merely sets up the action statements that follow:

" . . . staff will be reduced by 2.5 FTEs."

" . . . the Downtown Health Center will be opened."

" . . . 25 beds will be fully converted to a day surgery unit."

" . . . the Home Dialysis Unit will be fully operational."

Obviously, this simple statement of intent does not contain all the information needed on achieving the objective. It also is necessary to identify where the institution or division will be when all the work necessary to realize the goal has been completed.

The plan of action that will see the manager and the unit or department through the goal-completing process is an important element of the operation. Most of the follow-on energies must be devoted to the process of working toward accomplishment of the objectives. The plan of action helps those administratively responsible to see that appropriate activities are directed to moving the entity to the fulfillment of its mission and goals.

The use of a planning model helps shape the activity. This model can take any form but must contain all of the parts necessary to assure that it incorporates the cybernetic elements identified previously (Figure 1-2). The following should be the minimum components in the design of the model:

- specific objective
- performance standard

- interim time frame
- completion time
- results, exceptions, revisions.

All of these elements should come together to provide a logical whole planning document. Readers of the document should have no difficulty seeing clearly what the nurse manager is about and the precise pathway she intends to follow.

PERFORMANCE STANDARD

As noted, the nurse manager must know or learn what activities to undertake in order to achieve goals. It might be asked: What does such detailed planning have to do with the building of a financial plan and budget? The plan simply outlines the manager's objectives so the financial resources necessary to support it can be provided. The absence of these details can set a well-conceived plan off course so that it ends up either not doing what was intended or taking a direction not consistent with the institution's overall mission.

Performance standards are the planning devices designed to assure that such undesired circumstances do not develop. The standards are simply activity statements that indicate the steps that will be taken at a given time in the effort to reach a defined objective. They usually identify an action step in the process and the time assigned. These steps generally depend for the most part on the completion of one before moving to the next. There are times, however, when the steps are simultaneous, requiring the completion of several actions at the same time or in conjunction with each other. Through identifying these steps the manager and others responsible for carrying out the work plan can establish benchmarks that show how their individual and collective actions relate to a desired objective. Since a performance standard must be described clearly, it also becomes a central tool for assessing progress in the context of change.

At times, the objective-achieving processes relate specifically to progress in making some significant change in the organization. An integral part of good planning is the realization of the goal's impact on the change process. The process itself can measure change progress by using it as a monitoring tool. The performance standards can provide insight into how well the process is progressing and, even more specifically, its quality.

''Noise'' or difficulties in the achievement of any given step can alert the manager that there may be problems that need to be addressed before moving on to the next stage. Assessment of the success or lack of it on any specific performance standard helps produce an accurate picture of the department's particular situation. With this capability, the manager can adjust responses at the time problems occur without jeopardizing any of the other activities or the progress toward an objective.

Here again, performance statements should be brief and specific. They should contain no more than one statement and should specify the action that can validate each stage of the process. Performance should be easy to measure against the standard. Compliance with time parameters should be reviewed carefully; failure to meet the deadline for adherence to the standard or course jeopardizes the time factors for subsequent performance standards and perhaps the achievement of the goal itself. Skill at designing performance standards and matching them to time frames will come with practice. The use of a practical format can help make it easier (see Exhibit 1-1).

Each of the steps should follow in a logical sequence. Each step also should serve as a marking point for measuring progress. The process itself should help the manager identify variables that are disclosed as the activity moves along. Sometimes constraints and resources not apparent at the outset are revealed as the process exposes such conditions or circumstances. The role of the manager is to interpret these influencing factors and make decisions that will alter or adjust the anticipated outcomes.

TIME PARAMETERS

Time frames in this process are vital to the successful achievement of the objective. In the formulation of goals, this critical factor sometimes is overlooked, with the result that problems arise in achieving outcomes in a manageable time period. Time is the manager's most important resource. If it is not allotted carefully, it can be difficult to complete objectives in a timely fashion. The use of time parameters in working toward objectives helps the manager assess progress. Time also provides a realistic relationship between the work on completing the objective itself and tying in its achievement to the overall organizational goals. Each depends on the other. Sometimes the nurse manager can be co-opted by the immediate objective and forget that it is part of a larger whole. Maintaining a close watch on the time frame helps the manager realize that each individual objective has an end in itself: to help achieve the institution's long-range goals.

Time serves the needs of everyone in completing the objective. It focuses efforts related to goal achievement, helping the manager keep her team on course. Time also creates a sense of direction and mobility because it causes the participants to recognize that they do not have an unlimited amount of time to complete their work.

Exhibit 1-1 Sample Performance Standards

GOOD CARE HOSPITAL
4 WEST NURSING

Mary Jones, R.N.—Nurse Manager
6/1/90

Specific Objective	Performance Standard	Interim Time	Final Time	Results, Revisions
Implement a 6-week repeating staffing plan.	1. Quiz staff on interest, and support; get input on a 6-week plan.	7/10/90	10/1/90	1. Staff very supportive of new plan, would like 10-hour day, 4-day week if possible.
	2. Form work group to study the literature and do a data search for scheduling approaches.	7/30/90		2. Data reveal that a 4-day/10-hour plan is feasible with no increase in FTEs on the unit.
	3. Select a plan that meets unit needs and have staff review it for input.	8/30/90		3. Schedule is developed using new plan. Splitting 1 FTE into part-time positions is required.
	4. Develop and review with work group the costs of the selected staffing approach and prepare presentation to nursing administration.	9/15/90		4. Work group moved the part-time positions into weekend schedules. This allowed every other weekend off for full-time staff. Weekend differential cost will increase $435 per annum.
	5. Present to nursing administration for final approval.	9/30/90		5. Presented to nursing administration for annual budget consideration. It insisted that plan must offset overtime use by 10 percent in next fiscal year. The unit staff agreed.

Outcomes

Obviously, there would be no reason to accomplish objectives if there were no anticipated outcomes. This is the reason all objectives are formulated. Upon completion of all the steps in the operational process, the outcomes must be evaluated against the original objectives. Since the objective actually is a statement of anticipated outcome, it must be compared with the results achieved to determine whether continued support of the activity is appropriate.

Statements that relate to specific action steps are important in ascertaining whether they led in the direction of the anticipated outcome(s). Each evaluation statement in this phase of the process produces important information on progress. Items discovered through research, interim assessment, or action should be identified in this section. Data from here will influence the manager's conclusions as to further action and, ultimately, the organization's response in fulfillment of its objectives. It is here that the manager will find the information upon which further refinement will depend.

This information should be conclusive if the elements of the process have been described well and acted upon. It should make clear the need for future action. Completion of the objective often provides the basis of the design of new goals, responses, and actions, each taking the participants and the organization closer to their desired outcomes. This approach provides a continuing monitoring and controlling mechanism that keeps the organization on course.

This all lies at the heart of the financial process. The financial planning components should be directed toward defining these objectives in numeric terms. The resource allocation in this process should relate specifically to the viability of the objective. If it appears appropriate, the organization can make a financial commitment based on data, not as a shot in the dark.

UNDERPINNING THE OBJECTIVE PROCESS

Clearly, identifying an objective is not an isolated process. Other processes must be in place that operate to support the objective-setting activity. There are many indicators that the management planner must assess as cues to the appropriateness of an objective or plan developed by the institution. Information that reflects the climate for specific processes or programs and has an impact on their outcomes must be incorporated into the planning.

The manager must be alert to the state-of-the-art circumstances of the services for which the department or unit is responsible. Since health care technology changes rapidly, the manager should be aware of major developments in technology and services and should be prepared for discoveries that may have an impact on the services offered. Maintaining this informational base can be difficult and even challenging. The manager often feels overwhelmed by the amount of data and information available on these swift advances. Some of this information may appear contradictory or may not give a clear picture of where the health care industry is or might be going. It is here that the manager gathers what information is available, applies her best judgment, and draws a conclusion or series of assumptions upon which her decision will be based.

The manager uses a number of sources for validating her decisional data base. Focusing solely on her own field of service for the information can deprive her of essential data perhaps not available to her in a specific area of service or practice. The manager must expose herself to many sources of information. To the extent that she utilizes these resources, the effectiveness of her decisions and the efficacy of her plan will be enhanced or constrained. The following is a partial list of the kinds and locations of the data the manager may need for making effective planning decisions:

- Finance Office: Historical indexes, ledger data, balance sheets, fiscal projections, operating reports, profit/loss summaries, finance field data, economic indexes and forecasts, computerized gaming and assumption statements, accounts payable/receivable data, etc.

- Marketing Office or Service: Service surveys, demographic and geographic studies, service population reports, concept assessment, market design, market planning, consumer studies, market projections/analysis.

- Professional Data: Journals, technology information, new professional processes/procedures, national professional practice trends, research data, published impact reports, university-based studies, experiential practice reports.

- Internal Department Data: Service reports, staffing data, productivity studies, service mix data, expense summaries, service delivery reports, satisfaction surveys, internal finance data, departmental performance reports, etc.

- External Service Data: Physician performance profiles, case-mix reports, quality assurance studies, cost summaries, consumer reports, administrative reports, board of trustee reports, medical staff committee minutes, hospital committee minutes, previous goals, institution's annual report, etc.

These are just a sample of the types of information that may make up the manager's planning data base, but they give some idea of what is essential. The planner must be able to determine the influences that affect the work she does and the services of her department or unit. The more information she collects to support the plan, the more accurate it will be and the more likely it will reflect the direction of the institution and win the support of its officers at budget time.

Pulling all of this information together is a creative process (see Figure 1-3). It demands that the manager develop assessment skills in interpreting the data. Data are presented in many ways. They may be designed to be understood by those who will receive and interpret them for their own purposes. The manager may have to take data that appear almost incomprehensible to her and make sense out of them so she can apply them to other data and integrate all the information with the service

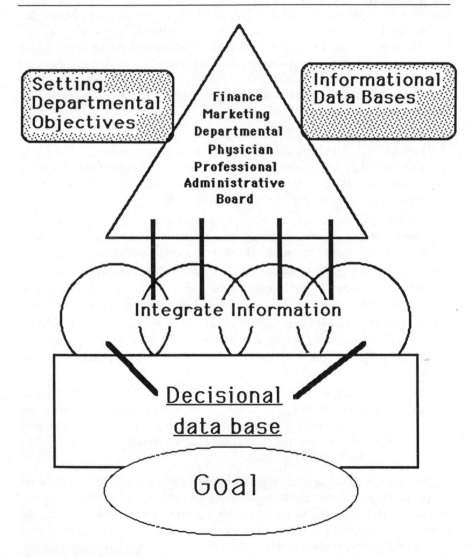

Figure 1-3 Goal-Setting Process

needs of her department or unit. She will find it helpful to call on the interpretive ability of the people for whom the data were intended originally.

Data for their own sake have little or no value. Understanding them can make a difference in the quality of the decisions the manager makes.

The manager in this process must be able to integrate the many data sources into a meaningful indicator of the appropriate direction to take. She thus discerns what goals can help stimulate the unit, department, or institution to move ahead.

GENERAL ASSUMPTIONS

The budgeting process determines the economic, social, and health care variables and indexes that may have a direct impact on institutional or program planning activities and can guide the manager's decisions. These decisions usually are the outcome of a collective process by the board and the administrative staff. It reflects a thorough assessment of the health care field, the economic conditions under which the institution will operate during the next planning period, and specific strategies the facility will undertake to respond to its unique service and market conditions (see Figure 1-4).

The manager then determines the implications of these general assumptions for her department or unit (see Exhibit 1-2). Individualizing them brings home to her their meaning and impact and their constraints and possibilities in the next operating period. She should incorporate them into her planning.

However, attempting to plan outside of these parameters is seldom helpful. If the assumptions do not support a particular goal of the manager even after it has been approved by her administrative superior, she and the administrator should resolve that problem promptly. Once that is done, the general assumptions should provide the guidelines for the manager's efforts in formulating her department or unit objectives.

Of course, there are specific departmental behaviors and activities that will need to be incorporated into the assessment so that the departmental plan can be adjusted to reflect realistically such factors as staff adjustments, physician changes, resource allocations, service adjustments, new programs, and services. This will provide a more definitive framework within which she can define her operational goals (see suggested form in Exhibit 1-3).

Clearly, the planning phase is the first, most fundamental, and most important in the financial process. Unless the health care institution and its departments and units have a clear understanding of how they fit in with and respond to the world around them, the financial activities will be in some disarray. The finance service merely polices the fiscal implementation of the institution's purposes and goals.

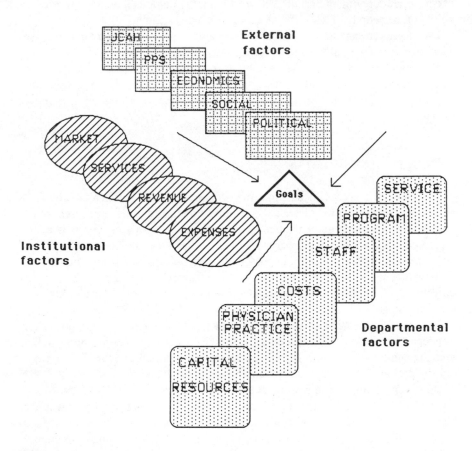

Figure 1-4 Planning Assumptions

The rules that govern good business management also apply to the health care industry. The new competitiveness and the need to be economically viable call for all the planning skills available to the business. The nurse manager, as with all managers in the institution, now must be a skilled business thinker and use business planning strategy as a part of her executive role.

A systematic and carefully structured planning approach that is used consistently by the entire institution is its best defense against competition, costly service errors, and inappropriate expenses. The ability to evaluate performance against established goals and objectives and to make critical decisions on future commitments and performance is essential to business survival in health care today and in the foreseeable future.

Exhibit 1-2 Sample Planning Assumptions for the Next Year

- No major changes are expected in regulatory activities.
- Prospective payment system payouts will drop about 1 percent.
- There will be no labor relations problems or union organizing activity.
- Strong stability is expected in the job market.
- The inflation rate will increase no more than 2 percent.
- There will be no increase in current staffing levels for existing programs and staffing for new programs will have to be justified.
- The institutions will make a renewed commitment to ambulatory and geriatric care and support services.
- Three additions will be made to the medical staff in the area of sports medicine (in the next quarter).

Exhibit 1-3 Sample Assumptions Format

PROGRAM ASSUMPTIONS
Name:_____
Department/Unit:_____
Date:_____
Planning Period:_____

Assumptions	Constraints/Resources Implications
Administrative Assumptions	
Economic Assumptions	
Service Assumptions	
Medical Staff Changes/ Adjustments	

SUGGESTED READINGS

Anthony, Robert, and David Young. *Management Control in Nonprofit Organizations*. Homewood, Ill.: Richard D. Irwin, Inc., 1984, 281–320.

Claus, K.E., and J.T. Bailey. *Decisionmaking in Nursing*. St. Louis: The C.V. Mosby Company, 1975, 15–16.

Drucker, Peter F. *Management*. New York: Harper & Row, Publishers, 1974, 130–58.

Finkler, Steven A. *Budgeting Concepts for Nurse Managers*. Orlando, Fla.: Grune & Stratton, Inc., 1984, 1–38.

New Age Information: Beginning with a Data Base

OBJECTIVES FOR CHAPTER 2

This chapter will:

1. *Identify factors that will create a new environment for financial planning.*
2. *Describe characteristics of the health care organization and its operating framework that have an impact on the financial resources and budget planning of the clinical manager.*
3. *Define the informational basis necessary for the nurse manager to undertake financial planning activities.*
4. *Identify sources of patient and service account reporting and processes for creating such accounts.*
5. *Introduce computer information systems.*
6. *Describe the kinds of data necessary to establish an information base for the nurse manager in her budgetary planning.*
7. *Clarify the need for data formats for the continuing collection of financial and budgeting information.*

New age finance is not arising as a singular event on the horizon of the 21st century. It's arriving at a time of many social and environmental transformations. These changes are driven by the many adjustments in the workplace and, more specifically, in the health care delivery system. As both worker and workplace adjust to these new societal influences, changes in information technology and its use are forming the system's response. Nursing, of course, is not exempt from these adjustments; in fact, it is at the heart of making them. All systems from today forward will require substantial flexibility and creativity.

The traditional approach to financing health care already is moving through a number of transitions leading to new and radical concepts in financial management that demand entirely different processes and responses. Corporate reorganizations are necessitating new ways of financing institutions, as well as different styles of management and ways of interacting.

Health care services are likely to be much more independent in determining and managing their own finances and to be more self-supporting. Corporate reorganizations and decentralizations will remove nursing from a central authority, assigning it the role of an independent corporate entity that relates to the overall institution through a contractual or similar link.

PRODUCT-BASED AND OTHER APPROACHES

The decentralized approach is likely to become the model for complex multiservice institutions offering a broad range of health-related and nonrelated services, such as investment companies, fast food services, insurance, and the like (see Figure 2-1).

It thus is clear that this transition is having a fundamental effect on the management of finance. Much of the budgeting process must be adjusted to reflect the many changes facing the nurse manager.

A product-based approach is more likely to be the standard than the exception. Financial outlays will depend more directly on services provided and related to their outcomes. The nurse executive must clearly identify the extent of commitments to achieve outcomes, validate the work to be done, then justify her expenditures against the benefits to the institution. Each unit or department of the nursing division will become a finance center operating in conformity with its defined standards and performance expectations. All of this will be evaluated against the defined outcomes and how well they are achieved.

Reporting and finance periods also will change. There is likely to be less dependence on the annual report because the reporting and data characteristics of the information services will be of such quality, frequency, and sophistication that details on performance as well as projections and/or assessments will be available much more quickly and for shorter periods of time, such as daily "at a glance" capsulized reports. Since the marketplace has become increasingly more competitive, the institution's ability to respond very quickly will be paramount to the success of any of its ventures. New and critical programs may be added to the institution's service array in far less time than ever before.

The multiventure health care corporation will be considerably more loosely structured than it has been. The nursing service will be a corporate arm that will develop a short- and long-term business plan like any of the other corporate divisions. This will bring more flexibility to the management of nursing—but it also will demand increased accountability. Productivity, outcome, role, and account-

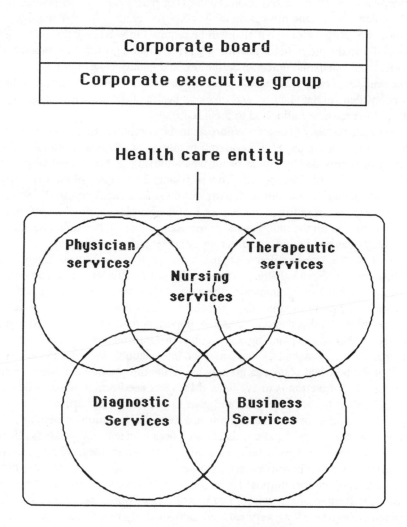

Figure 2-1 Multilateral, Interdependent Corporate Structure

ability all will be correlated more effectively and the corporation will expect work performance to reflect agreed-upon standards of practice and performance.

As noted, the nursing profession in the corporate entity will have more opportunity to be self-governing but also will be required to validate its role through a financially sound program for providing service. Shared governance, practice parameters and standards, outcome definition, and quality control will be inherent in the practice of each professional. Services that are not able to be self-sustaining or to contribute to the viability and financial health of the organization generally will find the resources allocated to them reduced.

The two key areas of concern to nursing in the corporate era are (1) the routine inpatient or institutional services offered by nurses and (2) the more individualistic services provided by nurses or for which nursing will be accountable. Both of these will require planning. The core of financial budgeting obviously is good business planning. Each unit or department must fit its activities to the goals of the organization, as outlined in Chapter 1. Business planning will be essentially the same process for the routine nursing services, whatever they might be; they do not simply mean bed-bound care. Everything nursing does must be subject to review in terms of the organization's approach to meeting its service obligations.

This clearly indicates that a service may be just as eligible for extinction as it is for development or continuance. The demands of the marketplace and the institution's goals will predominate, and the services offered will have to reflect those realities. All this demonstrates how important data are in the decisionmaking process of business planning. Clear, objective information, both retrospective and prospective, is essential—the better the information, the better the decision.

All of the best-laid plans can go nowhere if the information necessary to give them form and direction is unavailable. Managers need data to make solid decisions related to the work they do and plan to do. They must acquire data from appropriate sources or generate them themselves. Each institution obtains information pertinent to itself and consistent with both its needs and its goals. Unfortunately, however, many institutions tend to collect data they neither need nor want. Data collection becomes a process unto itself and often much of the material generated serves no real purpose for anyone and makes no measurable difference in the effectiveness of the worker or the workplace. Some data are produced at considerable expense for a very isolated individual or group because it is nice to know rather than necessary to know.

Every manager must make it one of her goals to identify the essential data required to do an effective job and then seek ways to make sure she can obtain them. Most of the financial process begins and ends here. All finance is built on the plans and data that support the work activities of the unit or department in carrying out the institution's objectives. The manager who has detailed knowledge of those plans and activities is better able to determine, meet, and evaluate her goal achievement.

Many nurse managers have fallen headfirst into the "just-in-case" syndrome. In such a situation, any and all data are maintained in the files—just in case they may be needed some day to validate or justify an action, proposal, or program. This kind of data collection wastes both valuable space and time. It comes out of a period in nursing's history when the profession had to hang onto everything it had or stand the chance of losing it.

There has been a strong "us–them" relationship between administration and nursing for years. However, as health care has become increasingly complex, with emphasis on integration of systems and services, many such strategies and behaviors must disappear. Integrated data bases must be developed that yield a wide variety of information on a number of resources in such a way that the data can give a clear picture of what has occurred already and some idea of the outlook in a specified area and service.

THE NEED FOR INFORMATION

The nurse manager requires specific information essential to providing any patient service. All data that relate to patient care must be identified and explored. Of course, she will need financial and departmental data from others to integrate with her clinical information in order to create an overall picture of the status of her operation.

Such statistical data can give her raw numbers that outline the nature and condition of her service and activities over a given time period. Most data collection begins with the compilation of raw statistics on patient population for the past reporting period. An appropriate data management period generally is two to three years. A span much longer than that stretches the boundaries of reality since the health care system is in a period of exceptional change and adjustment. The rapid turnover of information and system needs dictates an abbreviated data period. The market also is changing at an accelerated rate, so shorter and more incisive data reports and reporting periods have become the rule.

The nature of the work often dictates the kind of data the manager will need. The length of time that the work has been a part of the institution can make a considerable difference. If it has been a routine element for a long time and will remain so, the data needed will be different from those collected for a new or alternative service with dissimilar parameters. Good data management requires information in at least three areas: the market, the service, and the operation. Each of these is a piece of the whole. Individually, each gives a detailed view of its own operations that will help the manager make decisions. Each institution also has different levels of capacity for generating data. The manager must determine the baseline of data necessary to do her job. Her effectiveness will be measured for the most part by the detail and reliability of the information she has available, and how she uses it.

A word about financial and planning data made available to the nurse manager by administration, finance, and data processing: As indicated in Chapter 1, there should be few financial planning secrets in the organization; indeed, most such secrets are ludicrous and have little real value. The manager responsible for a defined area has a right to information that has an impact on her operation and its success. That does not mean merely data that reflect the activity of the service itself. She also needs data on the circumstances that have an impact on her service and affect it directly or indirectly in any way.

Sometimes the kind of data required will not be that usually generated for a nurse manager yet will be vital to a specific activity or decision. Those responsible for data generation must be flexible in their approach to its availability and for generating whatever the manager may deem essential for making accurate and timely decisions. The data thus must be developed and presented in a way that is viable and meaningful to the manager. Data systems should be so designed or made flexible that the user can rely on their accuracy, validity, and comprehensibility.

While the manager must focus on the three separate areas of data collection—the market, the service, and the operation—they are not necessarily totally distinct from each other. Integrating the information to provide an overall perspective is far more important than distinguishing what bits of data are market specific, service based, or operational. The manager in this case resembles an artist in her approach to data collection and management. She is assembling all the components of her information base in order to get a solid idea of the status of her service. She will merge some data from each or all three of the areas to obtain a complete, overall view of the situation.

In today's financial management process, the nurse manager may have to review data in many different ways. She may be required to:

- look at elements of the service and compare them with other elements
- review segments of her service singly or collectively
- view the service as a whole and make decisions on all of its components.

Varying levels of detail are required, all subject to the judgment of the manager. As she becomes more comfortable with the components of the data report, she will become more flexible in its use.

The key to all this is the content of data reports. Statistical data can offer a whole range of information that can be helpful to the manager. It is best, however, to arrange data into a program hierarchy. This approach best represents the program-specific and decentralized approach to financial management and planning. Each program is a complete representation of all the factors that go into producing and operating it, whether it be a specific diagnosis related group (DRG) category or a patient care program with its own special character.

It is reemphasized that across-the-board departmental budgeting that isn't service specific is likely to disappear as a financial mechanism within a few years because it does not provide the type of data needed for making market and account decisions. Each service or patient is essentially an "account"; management systems now and in the future will have to look at their services and performance in light of such accounts. The account data by now should constitute both the framework and the heart of information generation (see Exhibit 2-1).

Exhibit 2-1 Examples of Account Data Forms

PATIENT ACCOUNT
DRG Category_____
Service Category_____
Service Area_____

Services Received	Service Cost
Diagnostic	_____
Therapeutic	_____
Treatment	_____
Nursing	_____
Home	_____
Ambulatory	_____
Health Education	_____
Other	_____
Total	$ _____
Price of Services	$ _____
Net Gain or Loss ( )	$ _____

(see service reports)

SERVICE ACCOUNT REPORT
Service: Nursing
Patient Number: 12345567
DRG Category: XYZ

Services Received:	Service Cost
Personal Hygiene	$ _____
Therapeutic Care	_____
Patient Teaching	_____
Discharge Plan	_____
Family Teaching	_____
Home Nursing	_____
Ambulatory Visit	_____
Other	_____
Total	$ _____
Price Portion, Nursing	$ _____
Net Gain or Loss ( )	$ _____

Account management therefore is the financial process that guides the nurse manager. Skills in both planning and constructing accounts are essential, as is the ability to evaluate and take alternative or corrective action. While the basic components of the budget are uniform, there still is a need for human, material, and financial resources to get the work done. Melding these resources into an effective work plan and then managing them appropriately constitutes the continuing task of the nurse leader. The budgeting process then will involve putting together a mix of the proper resources to make the plan work effectively.

THE STATISTICAL DATA

In setting the stage for a viable work plan or business strategy the nurse manager needs two kinds of data: retrospective and prospective. Such data can be generated in a number of ways and from a range of sources. Since most of the services that nurses offer are patient related, this section focuses on financial planning for those services. These same processes hold true for other data sources for businesses other than patient care in which nurses are involved.

The first step is to identify the business in which the manager is involved. It is that business that will set the parameters of all the activity that will be undertaken to meet its needs. To make decisions as to the nature of the business and the direction in which she will take it to meet the needs of her market, the nurse manager must ask herself a host of questions, then find the data on which to act:

- What is the case mix or service population?
- What specific services do we offer?
- Who are our customers?
- Who are the physician providers?
- Who is the competition? Where?
- What is our performance history (if we have one)?
  1. number of cases
  2. case mix (kinds of cases)
  3. profitability
  4. demographics
  5. population
  6. costs
  7. service needs
  8. resource use (staffing/materials)

- What administrative commitment is there for this service?
- What percent is this service of the institution's bottom line?
- Is this service consistent with facility's business plan?
- Does this service integrate well with other services?
- Is this a lead service (will it lead to the use of other services)?
- Can this service be done effectively and economically?

These vital questions must be addressed before the financial planning phase is even considered. The answers put the service in perspective to help guide the manager in putting together an appropriate plan. Her awareness of the potential impact of the proposed service (or of current services) is key to assuring a viable program.

The availability of sources of data can be a concern. The health care institution should have in place a data-gathering service that obtains, integrates, collates, correlates, and interprets important service information for the organization's management team. In most cases this function is spread through several departments. The data services department should have most of the information managers need on the institution's operations. It also generates information for administration and unit management.

The data may be available directly to managers or may be limited to certain levels of administration. If the latter type of information is essential to the manager's functioning, she will have to obtain it from administration. Geographic, demographic, and community-based data often can be obtained from the marketing department or the unit that handles the marketing function. Such data inform the manager as to the population, service area, strategic plan, forecast, and other statistics on the service area.

The manager also should have her own departmental or unit data on the services offered, costs, profits, and other performance-related aspects. Information on the utilization of staff, materials, and supplies should be provided on a regular basis to help the manager meet her operational monitoring responsibilities.

When sufficient data have been collected and reviewed by the manager, a statistical framework must be provided and a plan formulated to give direction to the process of providing financial and other resource support that is to follow. Again, the manager must ask and answer some basic questions:

- When I integrate the data, what do they say to me?
- Are the data consistent with the direction of the organization?
- Are there sufficient data for me to make a decision?
- Are there adequate committed supporting physician providers?
- Are there sufficient other appropriate health providers?

- Do the data fit my own department's services, skills, and profile?
- Can the data help me implement the plan?

Some of these factors will be appropriate and others will not, depending on the service, placement of the department or unit in providing services, and the constraints in effect. The point here is that the manager must give as much consideration of these preliminary questions as possible because this is the place in the planning process where most of the decision-related risk and planning errors occur.

Based on whatever data are available, at this point statistical projections should be made as to the service(s) to be offered. This should be done with input from all department or unit members having any role in the planning process. The institution usually has some planning parameters available to help guide the manager. The administrator and the finance and data processing executives should have input if for no other reason than to assure a common understanding and acceptance.

This collective validation of the projections should provide confidence that the numbers reflect the best thinking of the institution. Subsequent doubting the numbers and seeking to place blame for errors is an exercise in futility and should not be permitted. Similarly, if the best-laid plans turn out to be inadequate, recrimination and retribution will do nothing to change the situation and should be prohibited. Instead, it is better to adjust the plan to reflect the situation more realistically.

Making service projections is a relatively straightforward task once the underlying homework has been done. If an existing service is involved, a review of its social, economic, policy, and practice variables should give a fair perception of whether its efforts have been appropriate. There should be a common framework in the organization for arranging data. Practice patterns of the primary service provider should also be taken into consideration so the resources provided match the services offered. The use of historical, current, or prospective practice projections will provide a sound baseline for determining resource allocation (see Figure 2-2).

It is essential to communicate with those directly influenced by or involved with the service projections. When projections are being incorporated into the business plan, input from physicians and other providers is vital. So, too, are the data information department or other services that can validate the projections in a statistical or marketing framework. Since the manager's whole financial plan will be based on these data, she must be assured that the numbers are valid.

The health care institution obviously has some framework for providing the array of data for a defined period of time—historically, a 12-month fiscal year. That is not always the most effective measurement period for the success or failure of a project or service. Some may take at least a year to penetrate the market and

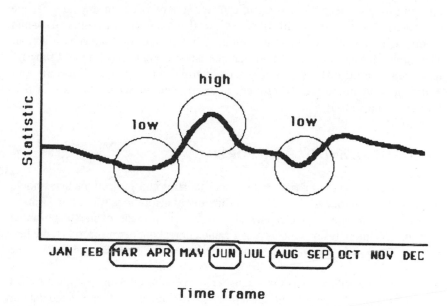

Figure 2-2 Nursing Practice Projections

Note: Projections reflect the practice behaviors of the primary service provider or the use pattern of the primary consumer. The highs and lows will require adjustments in the amount of resource use.

obtain measurable responses; they may take longer to reach a statistically valid use level or a profitability level. Any shorter time may lead to removal of resources before the service has time to pay off. Conversely, too long a period may be a waste of resources and time. Decisions as to appropriate time periods must be made carefully.

The quality of sophistication in both information systems and financial management now allows for a wide variety of program financing periods. The need for universal uniformity in reporting and budgeting periods may be long past in a corporate health care environment moving toward the 21st century. In a complex multilateral corporate structure that is market driven, the administrative and fiscal structures of traditional organizations will be modified to represent the market they serve. Cyclical budgeting strategies may be introduced into the structures. In these systems the budget period may be continuous, having no discernible beginning or ending. Reporting periods will be whatever is appropriate to the kind of service being offered and the variability in operation within the service. Reports may therefore be generated monthly, quarterly, semi-annually, annually, or even over longer periods. The more variable the service data, the more frequent the reporting requirements. When significant exceptions occur in any service, the computerized data system will "kick out" or flag them. It will even analyze and report their significance to the appropriate administrator or manager for action. The nurse manager now may find that she has different reporting and time requirements for the different services for which she is responsible. The variations will depend upon the service offered, its needs, and the characteristics of performance unique to it.

STATISTICAL AND DATA-REPORTING

A format that is appropriate for service statistics and projections also should have elements unique to the service. While many institutions use a standardized approach, it is not always meaningful or helpful to present all such data in that manner. The more refined the manager can be in making her projections, the better able she will be to evaluate them at the end of the performance period (see Exhibit 2-2).

Each service will have its own statistical projection division that must reflect the actual types of care offered. General and departmental patient-related data or numbers will not suffice. On inpatient units, in the past, it was appropriate to base projections on raw totals of census figures. However, the advent of federally mandated account-based budgeting now requires more refined, clinically specific payment measures, such as doctor- and case-specific information. The medical records requirements are becoming increasingly effective in assessing physician case behavior that reflects service performance and cost impact by physician, patient, and case.

The nurse manager must think and act within this framework because she, too, is assessing performance of her service by case. Since each category of patient or kind of case involves different outlays of human, financial, and material resources, she will have to evaluate needs and use to assure there is an equitable match between the resources expended and the returns (profits) to the unit, department, and institution. Where there are variances, the more specific the data generated regarding the location of the problem, the more refined and accurate the corrective response can be.

COMPUTERS AND DATA ANALYSIS

The use of computerized data bases and the generation of data as an outflow of computer processing is a common financial planning tool for nurse administrators and unit managers. The nurse of tomorrow must be increasingly comfort-

Exhibit 2-2 Service Projections Work Sheet

AMBULATORY NURSING DIVISION
Home Support Service
Reporting Period_____
Manager:_____

Month	Teach	Support	Intervene	Therapy	Aide	Other
1						
2						
3						
4						
5						
6						
7						
8						
9						
10						
11						
12						
13						
14						
15						
16						
17						
18						
Total						

Total_____

Note: Projections should be outlined in a service-specific format designed to refine the data into their component parts or activities from which charges and/or statistics can be obtained.

able with the use of machine and microcomputer technology in the application of her management role, especially in data analysis. The use of computers has been helpful in nursing because it allows the manager to bring together diverse kinds of information, integrate it, and create from that amalgam a picture of her nursing organization in a form that is consistent and organized.

Computers are especially beneficial in data generation and analysis because they integrate information in logical and systematic ways, particularly in the management of human resources. Since human resources constitute the largest segment of the nurse manager's financial planning and controlling process, utilization of integrated and computerized information is a central concern.

Planning the staffing and nursing care processes through use of microcomputers allows the manager to review data prospectively and retrospectively and utilize the information in decisions to maintain stability or to encourage new growth, development, and market response in an individual nursing unit or department.

Much of what is covered in this text is amenable to computer adaptation. The most important consideration for the nurse manager is to assure that the application of data to computer systems be organized in a systematic way. All of the elements related to staff budgets from full-time equivalents (FTEs) to nursing care hours have a distinct interrelationship. The microcomputer can organize data collection and presentation into an integrated information source.

There are many well-designed programs in the marketplace to assist the nurse manager in organizing her nursing departmental data so that it can be adapted easily to computerization, if she has not done so already, as most have. The institution itself can develop and adapt various approaches to data integration consistent with its own needs. The nurse manager must remember that in so doing she is responsible for assuring that all appropriate data sources can be developed and integrated consistent with the hospital's system. Much of the information presented in this book and other sources on financial planning and control provides a minimum number of data sets that might be organized in order to generate the essential information bases.

In most institutions, the financial services division selects the computerized systems, consistent with the needs of the hospital. The financial systems tend to have processes that support their own needs. The nurse manager must assure that the system includes the components essential for generating, monitoring, and controlling data that are meaningful to her. Since most of the hands-on work will be done by those not necessarily associated with the clinical service, the nurse manager must ensure that her needs are considered equally with those of other services and departments.

The following specific areas of nursing management lend themselves well to a computerized system. The nurse manager may find opportunities for linking each of these somewhat separate factors into a format in which information from one element of nursing management can be correlated with data from other nursing systems in order to establish an integrated basis for analysis.

Staffing

All of the components of the staffing system, from obtaining and distributing human resources to scheduling, lend themselves well to computerization. The format must reflect the needs of the institution and of the department. Each nursing department must have its own specific mechanisms appropriate to its staffing needs; those must be incorporated into the computerized system. The nurse manager, therefore, must be sensitive to all of the elements of the staffing process that have an impact on management control and on her budgetary resources.

Here is where major integration occurs. Since a majority of the resources made available to nursing relate to staffing, the utilization of staffing resources and the expenditures of dollars must be integrated. That can form a basis for analysis and a systematic approach to fiscal and human resource control.

Standards of Nursing Care

The clinical component must relate to financial processes. DRG-related and diagnosis-based nursing care standards must be developed in a data base that is integrated with both staffing and financial information. If the clinical activities can be quantified sufficiently to be correlated in the computerized system with financial and staffing data, an integrated data base can be developed on specific human resource costs for the delivery of nursing care. Through this process, a generic standard can be established for any given nursing service (or other service in the institution).

The next logical step is the establishment of a basic human resource-related cost framework that is linked to the staffing and the patient care delivery process. Nursing's computerized system then can provide a picture of the basic costs of delivering care.

This picture or data composite can provide meaningful information to the nurse manager as to the patient care delivery process, its relationship to the utilization of human resources, and the expenditure of financial resources essential to meet defined service needs.

Resource Budgets

Through the use of a computer-based system based on patient acuity, staffing, and patient care, the nurse manager can create a financial framework for the delivery of services. The framework in this case would represent per-unit costs of nursing care as indicated by patient acuity, nursing diagnosis, and DRG category. The kinds of care standards applied to the DRGs, nursing diagnostic categories, and other such considerations have an impact on the delivery of services. From those relationships, a budget can be established upon which the nurse manager can plan the financial framework for her service.

The use of historical data presented in the formats described provides the base for making judgments on the future delivery of care. Such variables as changes in physician relationships, hours of care, or nursing care standard, when mixed in the computerized system with the other components, can indicate their value to, and impact on, the financial system.

Quality Assurance and Control

In many institutions the quality assurance program or system is poorly integrated with some of the structural elements just described. The implications of staffing variables on quality of care certainly are clear to all practitioners. However, this often is not evidenced in the context of quality assurance programs.

Part of the problem is the inability to integrate quality of care indexes fully with the operational components. Quality obviously should be related closely to the standards prescribed. A computerized system can relate such quality indexes specifically to:

- structural standards such as staffing and the allocation of human resources
- practice standards such as those of patient care based on nursing diagnosis within DRG categories
- financial parameters for assuring that those structural and practice standards are achieved.

The relationship among these three factors and their impact on outcomes can be enhanced through a computerized approach. This process can provide a mechanism for monitoring and controlling variances to assist the nurse manager and the clinical practitioner in making decisions that will help keep the service consistent within the established parameters.

Through utilizing the technology of computer systems, the manager can build a practical data base for managing the delivery of nursing care at the unit or departmental level. The development of such approaches and responses to a financial planning system provides an important initiation into the entire financial process.

The nurse managers' ability to use a computerized system can close many of the gaps they have experienced in attempting to provide, integrate, monitor, and control budgets and to work within the financial planning process.

BUILDING THE BUDGETING PROCESS

As noted earlier, the whole financial planning process reflects the service that is to be performed. This is an application of the architect's credo of designing form to follow function. The goal is to (1) create a budgeting format that will best assist the service to be provided and (2) develop the best possible data base to indicate whether desired outcomes have been achieved and why (or why not) that has occurred.

Resource allocation must be the first consideration. The manager must know how much resources she will need to provide the required services. A systems approach must be developed to present an integrated view of essential resources for providing services:

Resource Planning Activity*

- Mission and Purpose
- Corporate Objectives
- Corporate Business Plan
- Department/Unit Business Plan

Service Projections*

- Data Collection
- Data Integration
- Data Interpretation
- Service Projections
- Projection Validation

Service Budget Preparation

- Resource Utilization
  1. staffing
  2. material and supplies
  3. utility
  4. systems
  5. information
- Capital Resources
  1. needs
  2. costs
  3. availability
  4. time and use
- Revenues (Income)
  1. payment available
  2. deductions
  3. debt
  4. net (pretax)
  5. earnings (profits).

*Issues discussed in Chapters 1 and 2.

The process of developing the budget is relatively straightforward when the appropriate data are available (see Figure 2-3). While the level of detail in a budget is great, the mechanics of the process flow logically when the basic information is available. Again, the budget's validity will depend in large part on the quality of the data already collected. Much of the meaningful historical data of continuing services will have been maintained for each department or unit.

Those data must be pulled together to support the direction of the budgeted activities. If the nurse manager has maintained an accurate data base in the previous financial period, the actual structuring of her budget will be a relatively mechanical process.

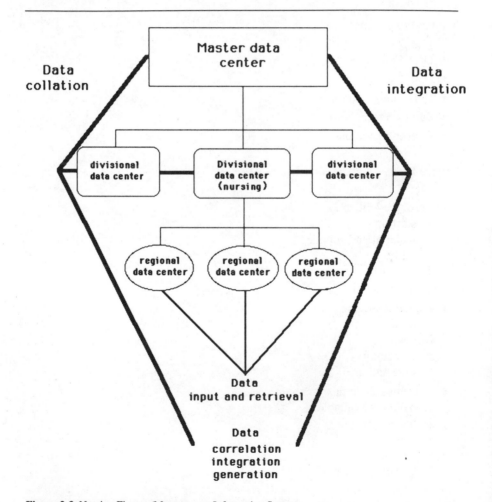

Figure 2-3 Nursing Finance/Management Information System

Services proposing new areas or reaching beyond their traditional client populations will find that the planning process will hold special importance and they will have to invest considerable time on it. At budget time, the groundwork will have been covered and the nurse manager simply will put pencil to paper.

In this case the initial budget will actually be a work plan that can be gamed or adjusted to produce different outcomes, depending on how the variables are adjusted in the computer. Gaming of business plans and financial plans is becoming more common. The "what-if" nature of this process allows the manager to look at her business plan from several angles and make adjustments to fit the variables or changes in the game (plan) to better reflect new circumstances, more data, expense limitations, etc.

This, again, points up the highly variable nature of program planning and why it requires a flexible manager and management approach. She will have to realize that there can be many variations on an original budget or financial theme and what she ends up with may little resemble what she started out with.

The budget process acquaints the manager with the hard realities of program planning. She may find that her best design, when all the pieces are put together, either does not meet the needs of the institution or costs more than its return can justify. The program can appear to meet a real need but the cost is prohibitive or there is little return value to the institution. More often, the apparent resource needs have to be adjusted more tightly than planned, requiring that much more of the same output be obtained with fewer resources. Some programs have to be scaled back, with the hope of expansion when the service returns lead the institution to increase its commitment.

The process of constructing a budget, as discussed, is like painting a picture—adjusting the scenes, hues, and colors as the work emerges. Only when it is complete can the quality of the work be assessed. The time invested in the preparation is most important. Eventually there should be some interface of nursing departmental data and the institution's systems so that newer and more effective data relationships can be established. This helps the nurse manager create the kind of information base she needs to make business decisions and adjust them as the data direct her.

Staffing, patient care, cost, economic, resource, and service data having an impact on the individual manager's operation when combined with broader organizational data can help in making decisions that can improve service delivery or reduce the cost of the service to both the institution and to the consumers. It can help the manager reduce her turnaround time between data generation and the impact of her decisions so that she can intercede quickly to affect the outcome if necessary (see Figure 2-3).

The manager of the future must be skilled at the manipulation and the flow of data. She must become comfortable with the language of data management so she can seek and obtain the kind of information that she needs for planning and controlling. This information base will continue to expand until most decisions become merely reflections of the data that guide them. The computer now can suggest decisions and the manager need only pick among a number of options and build the specific business plan to the option model selected.

It should be clear that the control, interpretation, and use of data and data systems is vital to management and fiscal success. Hospitals and health care facilities are generating a great deal of data and are creating efficient decisionmaking processes.

All financial planning depends on skills of review, interpretation, and application of information to decision making. As discussed here, understanding and application of detailed data resources and integrating them with other components is an important function of the nurse manager. From this base, the entire financial framework for the nursing operation grows and develops.

SUGGESTED READINGS

Anthony, Robert, and David Young. *Management Control in NonProfit Organizations.* Homewood, Ill.: Richard D. Irwin, Inc., 1984, 3–35, 357–427, 467–511.

Dillon, R.D. *Zero-Based Budgeting for Health Care Institutions.* Rockville Md.: Aspen Publishers, Inc., 1979.

Hoffman, Francis M. *Financial Management for Nurse Managers.* Norwalk, Conn.: Appleton-Century-Crofts, 1984, 103–17.

The Staffing Framework for Nursing Care

OBJECTIVES FOR CHAPTER 3

This chapter will:
1. Outline the determination of full-time equivalency.
2. Define unit of service and statistical determinations related to human resource management.
3. Clarify nursing hours per patient and unit of service statistics.
4. Discuss relative value units, patient care units, and patient classification processes.
5. Describe distribution of nursing staff to accomplish the goals of the unit or organization and review the development of a cost account framework.
6. Interface data and nursing management activities with the human resource planning process.

Perhaps the most extensive and expensive element in any health care programing is the cost of budgeting for human resources. It also is the most important factor because human resources constitute the nurse manager's greatest asset. In the final analysis, this resource provides the most valuable contribution to the program or services being offered.

Therefore, the human resource budget must be designed with the utmost care and understanding. In developing a program response to the financial plan, it is best to begin with some predefined standard or statistic that gives the manager some idea of the components of the service for which she must plan the people resources. The statistics usually are the unit of service and some unit of measure or performance (relative value unit) for delivering that care. This unit of measure usually reflects a time value for the service. Examples of this might be hours of care; minutes of procedure; care standard with time frames; number of tests per person, minute, or hour, etc.

The use of a standard becomes important when analyzing the budgeting processes at various times in the implementation phase. This is the area that gives most clinical managers the greatest problem. The standard often becomes simply the number of service units forecast, without any productivity level against which to manage the workload and associated human resource costs. Since these costs are a significant portion of the budgeted expenditures, they become important components of the nurse manager's variance analysis once the plan is implemented. Thus it is vital to develop this process both for preparing the budget and for analyzing it as it is being implemented.

In nursing there are as many statistical tools as there are services to be provided. However, they do have some common characteristics that any plan should contain:

- There must be a relationship between the unit of service and the unit of measure.
- The unit of service must always be a measure of function; the unit of measure must be an indicator of time.
- Both service and time must be references that can be related directly to the use of resources.
- There must be a financial value that can be related directly to both the service and the time it takes to provide it.
- Data collection devices should produce information that as clearly as possible inform the manager of the operating relationship between service and workload (unit of measure) in order to facilitate her response.

DETERMINING FULL-TIME EQUIVALENTS

This discussion of the human resource factors in developing a financial plan will refer to full-time equivalent units for determining the numbers of people required to provide the specific services called for in the financial plan.

Full-time equivalent (FTE) utilization is fairly standard in the health care industry as a unit for determining the position of a worker. It usually denotes a full-time work value or some portion thereof. Every human resource total (personnel or staffing) is calculated in terms of FTEs. This FTE classification usually represents 2,080 hours of work in a calendar year—that is, one person working eight hours a day, five days a week, for 52 weeks.

Exhibit 3-1 Full-Time Equivalent Determination

1 FTE = 2,080 hours per year, 40 hours a week for 52 weeks
Benefit Deductions:
          80 hours of vacation
          40 hours of sick time
          <u>64</u> hours of holiday time
Total   184 benefit hours
   2,080 − 184 = 1,896 FTE hours worked

In most health care institutions, that usually is the standard for defining FTE. Of course, most institutions do provide employees with at least a week a year (more likely two weeks) of time off as well as specified holidays. Therefore, these hours must be deleted from the original 2,080 total (see Exhibit 3-1).

The next step, usually is identified by the terms hours worked and hours paid.

HOURS PAID AND HOURS WORKED

The differentiation between hours worked and paid is important. Hours worked are the actual hours spent working; hours paid involve the total amount of time for which dollars are paid and always include all benefit time, whether or not worked. From the nurse manager's standpoint, hours worked are those needed to staff the unit or department.

The manager must develop a facility for using these two calculations interchangeably and for understanding their influence on budgeting and scheduling if she is to develop control skills for her role (see Exhibits 3-2 and 3-3).

All benefits time should be calculated in the same hourly terms, as is common in the workplace. If the workplace calculates the 40-hour workweek differently from the eight-hour-a-day standard, then that is the calculation that the manager must be use. Many institutions have staffing processes that break

Exhibit 3-2 FTE Factors

1,896 ÷ 2,080 = 0.91 FTE worked
FTE paid = 2,080 hours (with benefits)
FTE worked = 1,896 hours (without benefits)

   RULE: When calculating total cost of an employee, all benefits must be included. When calculating time available to work for scheduling purposes, only hours worked are used. This is true for all employee calculations and varies only if the benefits vary by employee.

Exhibit 3-3 Calculating FTE Worked/Paid Difference

Total FTE hours paid:_____
Benefit
hours: _____

                    _____   Paid hours − Benefit hours
                    _____   = _____Worked hours
Total   _____
Worked hours_____ ÷ Paid hours_____
= _____FTE worked factor

up the workweek into a number of different components. Whatever is chosen should become the basis for calculating both paid and worked hours. Other institutions still use the traditional eight-hour standard to calculate certain benefit days. Some have a standardized policy on paid time off that includes all benefit days. In those instances, the calculations must relate to the total time being identified in those plans. The manager should coordinate with the institution's human resources department on the best mechanism for nursing's circumstances.

SEVEN-DAY WORK WEEK

Inpatient services and some nursing and health care services may function on 24-hour days and/or seven-day weeks. That obviously affects the allocation of FTEs. The FTE remains the same but related factors change significantly. If the service must operate around the clock, that time must be covered.

It has been established that an FTE is a person who works five days a week for the entire calendar year. Hours worked have been identified and separated from total paid hours. The next step is to identify the additional components of an FTE that must be incorporated into the extended week to cover for those two additional days of activity that fall outside the scope of one FTE.

For every week of work on the seven-day schedule for each FTE, two days must be scheduled with additional work time. If five days is the weekly measure of one FTE, then one day must be one-fifth of that time, or 0.2 of an FTE; two days are 0.4, three days, 0.6, and so on. Therefore, for every one FTE, an additional 0.4 of an FTE is required to meet the needs of a seven-day schedule.

Exhibit 3-4 7-Day Work Schedule Calculations

5 days = 1 FTE.
Each day = 0.2 of an FTE.
2 time-off days per FTE = 0.4 FTE needed to replace.
Therefore, for every 1 FTE, an additional 0.4 FTE is needed to staff time-off days.
Every FTE position then needs 1 FTE plus 0.4 FTE in order to staff that position for a full
seven days (1.4 FTE).

This calculation is in addition to the FTE requirements to cover the benefit time. Benefit factors are specific to what is available to each individual division and must be calculated on the basis of the benefit time schedule in each situation (see Exhibit 3-4).

In the exercise in Exhibit 3-5, the nurse manager has an opportunity to apply the situation in her institution to the determination of FTEs. The manager should remember that the total number of FTEs is the sum of all the full and partial times in her service. Out of that she should delete the hours that are provided for benefits time, then determine the percentage value of that time and save it for future benefits calculations. Subtracting the benefits time from the hours paid results in the hours worked.

For the manager planning a program where there is no staffing history for calculating FTE numbers, much of this projection will be based on her having forecast service and workload parameters consistent with her planned activities (see Chapters 1 and 2). The relationship of unit of service to unit of measure will be the key to translating service and time statistics into FTE specifics. The mechanics are essentially the same. Hours of work per unit of service are simply translated into the standard FTE determinations acceptable to the institution or department. Reductions of benefit time and worked time follow.

Exhibit 3-5 Exercise in Determining FTEs

Number of current FTEs_____
Number of total hours paid_____
Number of total hours worked_____
Difference between hours paid and worked_____
Percent of hours worked of total hours paid_____
    (Hint: Divide hours worked by hours paid)
What implications do these figures have on planning the human resource budget?

UNIT OF SERVICE STATISTICS

Determination of statistics (units of service) and relating them to human resource budgeting is becoming increasingly important to nursing financial planning. The statistic is related directly to the nature of the service; it can be any item of activity that involves work and its potential changes. Historically, in nursing the unit of service has been used for staffing and record purposes but not often for charging. As nursing becomes more cost and revenue conscious and resource allocation an increasingly critical issue, establishing a relationship among unit of service, workload, cost, and revenue is vital.

Because of those implications for the future, this text bases its assumptions and practices on mechanisms to determine financial relationships among those factors and treats any nursing service as a revenue-generating entity. To do this successfully, it must be understood that all nursing activity has a significant value that either produces or uses resources. In any efficient nursing operation it is essential to maintain a reasonable margin of revenues over expenses. All management planning activity should be directed toward accomplishing this goal.

NURSING HOUR STATISTICS AND UNITS

The planning activity should determine how much service is to be offered by the department or service. Goals must be established before the nurse manager determines the resources necessary to meet such objectives. Whatever the goals might be—patients, visits, procedures, tests, etc.—the manager must decide on the number appropriate to the service, then establish a relationship between those units of service and the financial resources they generate and the resources they utilize.

After the appropriate units of service have been identified, it is necessary to (1) determine how much time is involved in performing the service (in order to calculate the human resource needs) and (2) allocate other resources to accomplish the work. (Those issues are discussed in Chapter 5).

At this point, the manager must ask: How much time will be required to carry out these activities to complete the work necessary to meet the goal of this service? Accurate historical data should be available from the computerized data base if this is not a new service. If it is a new service, it will be necessary to collect data from other like services elsewhere or turn to market data generated in assessing the viability of the program or through testing processes that assessed the amount of time it would take to perform the new service. In order to determine any kind of value, there must be some meas-

Exhibit 3-6 Nursing Hours per Statistic

Statistic: Visits, patients, procedure, unit, test, day, study, exercise, etc.
Hours: The amount of time that will be allocated to do the work indicated by the statistic.
Questions:
  1. How much work time does the statistic indicate?
  2. What is the work time committed to each statistic and to the total work to be done (6, 8, 10, 12 hours)?

---

urement viability to the time values assigned to carry out each unit of service (see Exhibit 3-6).

Time units are especially valuable in determining value. Since the primary professional service nurses offer is their skilled time, that time should provide the basis upon which economic and work value will be based.

RELATIVE VALUE UNITS/PATIENT CARE UNITS

Industrial engineering processes have introduced the use of relative value units for breaking down nursing activities into components of time within which the activities can be measured and correlated. Relative value units and patient care units establish a relationship between time and work. They have been used as units of measure in inpatient settings and are proving useful in relating services to cost and revenue and determining their impact on resource use and generation.

Effective data management is a key to success in building and controlling a financial plan. Financial planning projects available data into the workplace of the future (for whatever the planning period may be), leading to either success or failure. Accuracy and dependability of data can make a major difference in the viability of any enterprise.

The building of projections for both service and resource use should begin with the service numbers (such as cases) for which staff will be needed. This also is the first step in developing the data base for budgeting (see Chapters 1 and 2).

Once the manager has determined the unit of service (statistic), she assigns some work value related specifically to her service. As noted earlier, the manager must reduce the unit of service to its most effective level of measurability.

In budgeting in the past, it was acceptable in nursing to identify broad categories of service, often following the medical divisions of care delivery. This was in keeping with physician-based service allocations. In current and future nursing, this kind of identification is far from adequate. Units of service must be identified in terms of nursing-based expenditures of time so as to account accurately for work done and the time spent in doing it.

This takes on importance when the manager realizes that she and the nursing staff have considerable control over the kind and cost of services offered to each patient.

Whatever the units of measure the manager determines are appropriate, they should be clear, accurate, and meaningful to the staff. A unit of measure that has meaning only to the manager will suffer at the hands of a staff that neither understands it nor can use it effectively. Nursing patient classification systems, which define nursing time available for patient care, are a classic example of this problem in many institutions. At a time when they can be valuable for determining nursing value (unit of measure), they often have lost credibility with the nursing staff because of their inaccuracy and inappropriateness for daily staffing. Staff members thus must have a major role in the formation of any units of measure that will influence the determination of the work they accomplish and the value of their time.

Whatever unit of measure is adopted, it must be an objective representation of the value of the time it takes to accomplish a task. The use of relative value units has grown in the health care industry because of their objectivity and facility for determining dollar value; as mentioned, their use has become an important industrial engineering tool for allocating work/time relationships. The manager would do well to investigate this process with her institutional industrial engineer or several of the many texts on the subject.

This discussion, as noted, uses a relative value unit for allocating time value of nursing activity (units of measure). This patient care unit (PCU) identifies units of time encompassing all nursing activities. For purposes here, each PCU arbitrarily is assigned a time value of six minutes. In the real world, the time values of the relative value units are determined through work flow evaluations, time and motion studies, or other appropriate measures.

The time value of each unit of measure is the basis upon which the number of minutes or hours of nursing time is determined for calculating the use of human resources. Totals of the time allocated per unit of service give a summary of the total time spent in delivering a specified service. This process forms the framework for creating a particular nursing service account. These times are very important for providing the manager with basic information that, when correlated with the unit of service data, identifies how long (by hours) it takes to perform the activities.

From these bases, the nurse manager establishes the data base for determining the cost of the time she has allocated for the specified service. This, too, is per unit of service (in this instance, cases) and in given time periods (usually monthly). This data base should give the manager every month an idea of how many units of service and how much time (in this case, PCUs) per unit of service will be needed. Later, she will associate the cases and time values with individual patient accounts.

After determining the standard times for each case, the manager must multiply all cases by the time provided for each case in order to determine the total amount of time required. This must be repeated for every kind of case for which she is planning to offer services. Therefore, she must know not only her specific case mix but also the work time necessary.

In determining the appropriateness of services and the allocation of responsibilities, the manager of the future also must understand the divisions of accountability between the technical and professional workers in nursing. Those determinations are becoming a central issue for nurses. There also must be breakdowns on the number of technical and professional resources necessary.

Exhibit 3-7 presents the departmental statistics as historical data upon which the manager will base projections. In the example, a standard of performance expectation (5.5 hours of nursing care) has been suggested for the current fiscal period. The total PCUs have been identified and multiplied by their value factor (6 minutes per PCU) to obtain the total minutes of nursing

Exhibit 3-7 Departmental Inpatient Statistics

Care of Patient With Gastric Surgery
Four West
Dr. J. West
Current Standard: 5.5 hours of nursing care

Mo.	Cases	PCUs	Time	Hours	R.N.	Tech.	Var.
Jan.	26	51,480	8,580	5.5	4.4	1.1	0.0
Feb.	32	69,760	11,627	6.1	4.9	1.2	0.6
March	24	44,400	7,400	5.1	4.1	1.0	(0.4)
April	30	64,500	10,750	6.0	4.8	1.2	0.4
May	23	47,840	7,973	5.8	4.6	1.2	0.3
June	22	48,620	8,103	6.1	4.9	1.2	0.6
July	20	40,000	6,666	5.6	4.5	1.1	0.1
Aug.	25	49,975	8,329	5.6	4.5	1.1	0.1
Sept.	32	63,360	10,560	5.5	4.4	1.1	0.0
Oct.	34	66,980	11,163	5.5	4.4	1.1	0.0
Nov.	33	65,010	10,835	5.5	4.4	1.1	0.0
Dec.	29	58,290	9,715	5.6	4.5	1.1	0.1
Totals	330	670,215	111,701	5.7*	4.5*	1.1*	0.2*

*Average.

time utilized to provide services during the data periods (in this case, months).

When these minutes are divided by the units of service (patients, cases, and so forth) per month and multiplied by 60 minutes (to translate into hours of care), the real-time hours of care per case is identified. When this is further broken down into the time allocated for technical and professional nursing services, the manager obtains a clear picture of the activity in this sample. This format is repeated for every kind of case for which services are offered in the department or unit. The figures at the bottom of the last four columns Exhibit 3-7 also represent the average (mean) hours per case, producing an accurate measure of performance for the manager to compare against her standard.

This rather general data picture serves as the data base for making projections for the next fiscal period. Many of the indexes may be adjusted. Intensity measures (acuity, as measured by number of PCUs) may require adaptation at various times during the fiscal period. Case-mix numbers may change as provider or consumer circumstances change. Revenue demands and cost parameters also may change and these too, would affect the relationship among the data variables.

This development of a data base should be conducted in all of the cases offered by each nursing service, regardless of what care is involved or where it is provided. While this example involves a traditional case, the same formulas apply for any setting. The manager need merely adjust the terminology and service specifics to suit her situation.

A total review of all the service items should give the manager some sense of either (1) what human resources have been used as a data base for the next financial period, or (2) if such history is lacking, what data projections and forecasts are required to establish the personnel needs for the period.

As each clinical data base is reviewed, the manager can form assumptions for future planning. Assembling all the components of the planning process, she can create the human resource base necessary to accomplish the work (see Exhibit 3-8).

In the exercise in Exhibit 3-9, the reader is challenged to put together her data base for any specific service item. If possible, she is encouraged to take the time to do it for all her clinical service areas. She must determine the relationship between the unit of service and the unit of measurement (workload measure, time factors). From this she can obtain a relatively complete picture of the processes that comprise her informational data base. In Exhibit 3-9, the nurse manager compares her actual staffing (hours of care) performance with the standard determined for each care category (cholecystectomy, traumatic bowel injury, and so forth) and determines the variance between them.

Exhibit 3-8 Surgical Nursing Care Service and Case Summary

Care of Patient With:	*Actual*	*Stand.*	*Var.*
Cholecystectomy	5.3	5.4	(0.1)
Repair traumatic bowel injury	5.9	6.0	(0.1)
Large bowel resection w/o colostomy	5.4	5.5	(0.1)
Large bowel resection with colostomy	5.8	5.8	0.0

Note: Every specific care process identified will fit some category of identification (DRG, nursing diagnosis, relative intensity measure standard, etc.). Whatever that is for the nursing service should be the statistical unit upon which the budget parameters will be built.

Following the establishment of the information framework, the nurse manager must translate those data into meaningful time increments that can help her determine the number of FTEs she requires to staff the service. That means mathematically calculating total direct care hours from the PCU for a case. The number of cases, multiplied by the PCU value, produces the total PCUs utilized. This is divided by 60 minutes (as indicated earlier) to arrive at the total hours per case (see Exhibit 3-10).

In the exercise in Exhibit 3-11, the manager calculates her hours of direct care (or activity) to identify the unit of value for eventually determining the number

Exhibit 3-9 Statistical and Workload Projections Exercise

Unit Statistic:_____
(case, procedure, care item, etc.)
Workload Measure:_____
(hours of care, minutes, visit times, etc.)

Reminder: Reduce all your units of measure (statistics) and your workload measures to the smallest parameters possible. This allows for more accurate calculations and more refined budget categories.

Doctor:_____
Number of Cases:_____
Kinds of Cases:_____ Number_____
_____ Number_____
_____ Number_____
_____ Number_____

Units of Measure per Case:
Cases:_____ Nursing Hours per Case:_____
_____ _____
_____ _____
_____ _____

Exhibit 3-10 Calculation of Nursing Time

Statistic × Unit of Measure × Time
Example:
    24 Cases × 84 PCUs per case = 2,016 Total PCUs
    2,016 Total PCUs ÷ 6 PCUs per minute = 336 minutes
    336 minutes of work time required ÷ 60 = 5.6 hours
Therefore:
    It takes 5.6 hours of nursing time per case to deliver the required care for these cases.

of FTEs. Those hours will translate into FTE values (see Exhibit 3-12) that can be used to determine human resources needed and the cost of providing them (see Exhibit 3-11).

TRANSLATING HOURS OF SERVICE INTO FTEs

While it is not essential to work with breakdowns by FTE, it has become the practice of preference in most health care institutions. It provides a common language and process in personnel management that address a broad cross-section of human resources. To make the translation, simple mathematical procedures are necessary (see Exhibit 3-12), converting hours of service into FTE categories.

The number of positions required to do the work depends entirely upon how much time is considered the service's work period. In nursing, the work periods vary greatly to address the differing needs of the workers and the workplace.

Where a standard exists, the nurse manager converts her total hours of care, multiplied by her total units of service, into FTE positions. The product of that multiplication is divided by the number of hours in the usual work standard. If that is eight hours a day, then the product is divided by eight. The product of that division indicates numerically the number of FTEs required to deliver the number of hours of service to the units of service (see Exhibit 3-12).

Exhibit 3-11 Determining Hours of Direct Care

Cases, Procedure, Visit, etc:_____
Unit of Measure (workload):_____
Time Value of Unit of Measure:_____
Time Value in Minutes or Hours:_____
Remember: You are looking for *your* unit of value and a measure that reflects your nursing activity, whether that be visits per hour, hours per patient, minutes per procedure, etc.

Exhibit 3-12 Translating Hours into People (FTE)

$$\frac{\text{Units of Service} \times \text{Units of Measure}}{\text{Hours of Work}}$$

Example:

$$\frac{24 \text{ Cases} \times 5.6 \text{ Patient Care Hours}}{8 \text{ hours}}$$

$$= 16.8 \text{ FTE Nursing Staff Positions}$$

DISTRIBUTING THE STAFF

Once the manager has determined the number of FTEs required to provide the service, she identifies the distribution of the staff among categories and over the appropriate work periods. If the service works eight hours a day, five days a week, the shift distribution is simple. However, if there is seven-day service over 24 hours, the process is more complex.

In either circumstance the distribution between professional and technical workers will one day have to be determined. The division of role responsibilities between these two categories should be clear before this occurs. The percentage or ratio between the professional and technical positions should be determined by the unit or department practice standards, role requirements, and resources in the planning or objective-setting phase of the process. Based on those factors, the mathematical process that pinpoints the number of technical and professional resources is clear: The manager simply multiplies the total FTEs by the percentage of distribution in each category.

When there is more than one work period during a day, the manager must distribute the staff members across the number of shifts required. This distribution should not be an arbitrary factor; instead, it should reflect workload requirements as assessed over the entire work span. A nursing industrial engineering assessment of the key activity patterns upon which relative value units and patient care units are based, and workload indicators should identify for the manager what the shift outlay is. Based on those clinically engineered statistical compilations, a work distribution ratio is outlined. A percentage of distribution of staff over each shift of work will indicate the most appropriate spread of resources over the work day (see Exhibit 3-13).

Exhibit 3-14 demonstrates how the nurse manager can determine the number of FTEs needed and their distributions over three shifts. If she has different standards, they should be substituted for what appears in the exercise. The mathematical processes are no different for one, two, or three work shifts. This also holds true for more categories of worker than the technical-professional division outlined here.

Exhibit 3-13 Staff and FTE Distribution

Staff Distribution	FTE Distribution
16.8 Nursing Staff Members	
80% Professional Staff	13.4 Professional Staff
20% Technical Staff	3.4 Technical Staff
45% Day Shift	6.0 Professional Staff
	1.4 Technical Staff
30% Evening Shift	4.0 Professional Staff
	1.0 Technical Staff
25% Night Shift	3.4 Professional Staff
	1.0 Technical Staff

The manager should not include clerical and support personnel in the FTE determination at this stage of plan development. They are identified later when support human resource decisions are made. It is important to keep direct care costs separate from other associated costs so both can be identified and controlled more effectively (see Exhibit 3-14).

SALARY AND WAGE DETERMINATION

After the basic mathematical calculations have been completed, the number of FTEs determined, the category of personnel identified, and the work shifts with the appropriate numbers of personnel outlined, basic salary calculations can be made.

In most institutions, this process is handled entirely by the personnel division. Most of the data that nurse managers need for salary calculations can be obtained

Exhibit 3-14 Calculating Number of FTEs and Staff Distribution

_____Cases (or other statistic) × _____Unit of Measure	
Hours of Work (8, 10, 12, etc.)	
Shift Distribution (%)	Staff Distribution (%)
_____ Day	_____ Professional
_____ Evening	_____ Technical
_____ Night	_____ Other
FTE Distribution	Staff Distribution
_____ Day	_____ Professional
_____ Evening	_____ Technical
_____ Night	_____ Other

either from the personnel office or completed by that unit, depending on the facility's policy. Every manager should have a clear perspective of what has gone into such decisions and should understand the mechanics well enough to undertake the process herself should there be a need.

Determining salary cost depends on the total number of full-time and part-time equivalents required to do the work, their salary scales, adjustments or merit awards, and the timing in the fiscal year of such changes. It then is easy to determine the cost of the nursing services provided. The nurse manager should have a format for outlining the distribution of salary changes; most institutions do have formats for spreading these factors across the fiscal year.

The subsequent process is a simple mathematical procedure, multiplying the hourly rate by the number of hours, days or months worked. The manager notes when salary adjustments are to occur and implements them at the appropriate time. The calculation also includes the differential rate for shift, on call, or other classifications. These should be calculated separately and added to the base rate totals to keep them apart from benefit calculations that may depend solely on the base rate. Benefit and worked time calculations also should be kept separate so they can be accounted for individually.

Most institutions have computerized systems that will perform all these functions automatically. Where such systems are lacking, the manager should maintain records that break down these components into their individual parts and thus build a manageable control operation (see Exhibit 3-15).

DEVELOPING A COST ACCOUNT FRAMEWORK

The nurse manager must create a financial planning process based on accounts showing the costs of service to the patient. In this way, she develops a mechanism that links expenses and revenue and demonstrates their relationship.

Salary and wages can serve as an example, to show the relationship that the manager needs to establish with all components of the financial plan in order to monitor and control it at its most fundamental level. Each account should present a clear picture, both prospectively and retrospectively, of the activity that relates to that account.

The planning phase should establish a framework of expectation for behavior within the account. It should be clear to the manager and her staff what the performance expectations are in relation to both role and cost. Those expectations then should be validated against actual performance and its adequacy evaluated. A flexible financial system should contain a built-in mechanism for account adjustment to provide a process for corrective action.

The process of account building establishes a working relationship between the case (or other designation), the care standard, the costs of care, and the time over

Exhibit 3-15 Salary and Wage Determination

Professional Hourly Rate
 × Number of FTE hours worked
 + Number of hours of benefit time
 + Differential payment (if any)
 = Salary and wage cost per hour of care per statistic.
Example:
 $10.50 (hourly rate) × 1,896 (hours worked)
 + 184 (benefit hours) × $1.00 (hourly differential)*
 = $23,736 per professional FTE.

 *In this case, the differential is calculated only on hours worked, not on hours paid,
 which would include the benefit hours not actually worked on a shift for which a differential
 had been paid.

which services were provided. In this way, each patient has a framework of activity and cost that are identified solely with the individual and relate the specifics of work and cost unique to the clinical situation involved.

It is important to remember that the patient is involved in more processes than nursing alone. Other services generally are elements of the service and cost framework. The nursing portion would be an integral part of the array of accounts that specifically identified services for which the patient was charged directly and articulates not only what those services were but how much they cost and how closely (or otherwise) they related to the service and cost standards. Initiating the salary and wage costs of specific services by projecting them directly to the particular cases is the first step in creating an operational picture of performance expectations (see Exhibit 3-16).

Again, it is important to point out that a good historical data base is essential. Even if the service being developed is new, the planning should in-

Exhibit 3-16 Cost per Unit of Service

Kind of Case: Care of a patient with nasogastric tube feeding
Care Standard (time): 5.4 hours of nursing care
Direct Time Costs: 5.4
                     × 80% professional time ($)
                     × 20% technical time ($)
                     = Per diem direct care cost.
EXAMPLE:
  4.3 × $11.50* = $49.45 (professional time)
  1.1 × $8.50* = $9.35   (technical time)
     Total   = $58.80 (per diem direct cost)

 *assumed hourly rates for category

clude creation of an accurate data base upon which future activity can be built. The nurse manager is always refining her information base because that is what guides her in establishing a high-quality decisionmaking process for managing her business plan effectively, including assessing her service and assuring its viability.

From this basic framework the nurse manager establishes the parameters of the direct care cost base for each case or other unit of service. She has a picture of what each case should look like and the expectations of performance that will carry out the services. Her account record of services should match her per-case service plan in both format and content. The manager should be able to put them together and draw a direct daily comparison of the planned and actual service. In the best of all possible worlds they would match closely; however, that seldom, if ever, occurs.

The manager thus should use the plan as a guide to assess the performance as shown in the account and identify any disparities between the plan and its implementation. The variances should lead her to make decisions to improve the plan and to eliminate those differences.

The patient account plan should give the manager and staff a total picture of the service outlay. Service requirements inevitably will vary from the business plan over a given time. The variances will depend on the circumstances of the client and the service. The potential for such variances should be incorporated into the business plan to help evaluate a specific service in terms of direct care costs (see Exhibit 3-17).

In that Exhibit, it can be seen that the variability in intensity (as seen in the range of nursing care hours) is built into care of the patient following cholecystectomy. The difference in direct care costs as they relate to that variability, also is identified. While not cited in this example (Exhibit 3-17), the computerized system (and, with more difficulty, a manual system) would identify the professional and technical per-day direct care costs. Totaling these care hours, both consumer and staff can ascertain the service and the cost that comprised the nursing care provided over a given period.

It should be remembered that the relative value units that reflect the time factors for the elements of care activity for any given service can break down these costs more specifically and relate them to the discrete activities for which both time and cost have been determined. This is important in evaluating work and costs and in making adjustments when variances become unacceptable. The point here is that the manager will have a continuum of refined and accurate data that can help her plan for the coming fiscal year as well as develop monitoring devices to show how the service is performing.

The total direct personnel cost is identified when the hours of service are divided daily into professional and technical categories and the appropriate salary costs are identified for each day (see Exhibit 3-18).

Exhibit 3-17 Per-Account Direct Care Costs

Care of Patient After Cholecystectomy

Days of Service + Direct Care Time per Day
= Direct Care Costs per Account
EXAMPLE:

Days:	Nursing Care Time: Hours
1	4.9
2	5.3
3	5.6
4	5.6
5	5.1
6	4.6
Totals 6	31.1

Cost Calculation:
   31.1 × 80% (professional time) = 24.9 hours
   31.1 × 20% (technical time) = 6.2 hours
   24.9 × $11.50 = $286.35 (professional time)
   6.2 × $8.50 = $52.70 (technical time)
   Total account direct care cost: $339.05

Exhibit 3-18 Sample Patient Care Account

Care of Patient After Cholecystectomy

Nursing Costs Per Day

	Professional	Technical	
Day 1	$45.08	$8.33	
Day 2	48.76	9.01	
Day 3	51.52	9.52	
Day 4	51.52	9.52	
Day 5	46.92	8.67	
Day 6	42.32	7.82	
	286.12	52.87	Total: $338.99

Indirect Nursing Costs:
   Clerical: $46.75
   Departmental: 27.63   Total: 74.38
Material and Supply Costs:
   Equipment: $123.53
   Supplies: 262.43   Total: 385.96

                              Total Nursing Cost: 799.33

Note: This is the nursing portion of the patient or service account. It is integrated with other service and business data bases to create the complete account picture of the patient's service charges.

As the account is developed further the associated costs of nursing care support can be identified and added to the list. Indirect costs such as for clerical services can be accounted for on a flat rate per day or an intensity rate, depending on the clerical time spent on an account. The costs can be recorded in the same manner as nursing time. Indirect costs must be kept separate from nursing direct service time since their characteristics are different. The financial evaluation of care needs no other parameters. This allows the manager to determine the intervention and care components of clinical activity and their costs.

This same process holds true for other associated costs. Departmental and overhead costs that include management and utility expenditures and materials charges can be included here if that is acceptable to the institution. Most facilities allocate material costs to a central material services department and assigns them to a cost identification component for that department. Each of these considerations should reflect the operating behavior acceptable to the individual health care facility.

When the account plan is complete, each member of the staff should have a clear idea of what it contains. The total projected costs should be reflected, broken down into their component parts by day and by service provided. The projected figure should include all the costs associated with the nursing care delivery involved. In this way, when the total units of service (cases, etc.) are added, then multiplied by their individual expense totals, the manager has the total direct and indirect cost projections for the next fiscal year. In this framework, the human resource service costs are identified and related to the care provided.

THE SERVICE-HUMAN RESOURCE INTERFACE

This chapter has described the development of the human resource component of the financial business plan. The focus has been on providing a basic, systematic approach to developing the staffing involved in the direct nursing services. This has involved utilizing skills identified in Chapters 1 and 2 related to the planning process and applying them to the provision of human resources.

While the specific mechanics of this process are unique, the principles of the planning process apply also to the personnel component. The manager's role is to integrate the planning elements into the mechanics of human resource provision and create a framework that will project the needed resources accurately yet also will serve as a data base for future decisions on the appropriate provision of personnel to meet a defined need.

By reviewing statistical data of many kinds as applied to the service, putting together the account parameters, and providing for opportunities to monitor activity, the nurse manager builds a framework for effective operations in her

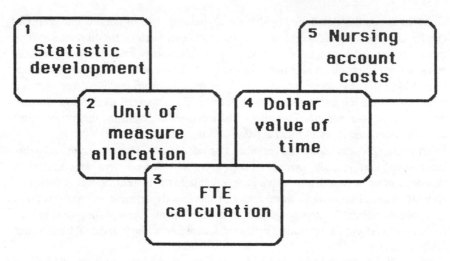

Figure 3-1 System Flow of Human Resource Budgeting

department or service. Each piece of the process must relate to the other pieces (see Figure 3-1).

As indicated previously, the process of financial management in clinical service is undergoing a metamorphosis. Nursing and other clinical services are trying to develop a system that can meet the demands upon it yet be responsible to the service population. This is tantamount to walking a circus tightrope with no net.

There are no presets on which to model a market-driven nursing finance system. As a result, the manager often will feel alone, just as though she were pioneering something never before attempted. The nurse manager has information and tools provided by the business community for establishing a planning and accounting system. Where possible, those processes have been applied here.

The largest effort, however, will be in the nurse manager's transition to a new way of thinking and operating. Her service is her business, and the strategies of all business apply here. That conceptual framework for thinking and behaving in itself will stimulate the manager to develop business approaches that enhance the work she is doing and provide the information she needs to assess it and, if necessary, do it more cost-effectively.

SUGGESTED READING

Smalley, H.E., and J. R. Freeman. *Hospital Industrial Engineering*. New York: Reinhold Publishing Co., 1984, 48–58.

Programming for the Human Resource Budget

OBJECTIVES FOR CHAPTER 4

This chapter will:
 1. *Outline the development of the human resources financial plan.*
 2. *Review the fiscal components of the financial budgeting process for human resources.*
 3. *Discuss the specific mechanisms for determining the assignment and distribution of work-related nursing hours.*
 4. *Explore the implications of special nursing divisional programs such as clinical and career ladders and their impact on the budget process.*
 5. *Provide specific tools for the nurse manager to practice the activities related to human resource budget planning.*

The first three chapters provided a conceptual and operational base for the processes associated with financial planning and development. Next, the focus turns to the practice of budgeting for a program. The presentation of the mechanics of the budgeting process is designed to provide the primary tools for this process.

STATISTICAL DEVELOPMENT

As noted earlier, the fiscal periods for planning in the future will reflect more closely the needs and the specifics of the plans and the activities they outline. Many new projects and proposals will take more or less than a year, depending on the nature of the service and the characteristics of the development process. For purposes here, the analysis will center on annual time segments. This helps provide both consistency and focus.

Statistical development is a major key to the success of the planning process. The statistical elements break down into measurable, numerical components that indicate the total service items that will be addressed within the given period. Each nursing setting will need the mechanism that best displays these items. Whichever format is used, it should at least identify the statistics by name and number and array them over the appropriate service period (see Table 4-1).

DEVELOPING A HUMAN RESOURCE FINANCIAL PLAN

The nurse manager must put together a financial picture of the utilization of the human resources over the plan year in terms of the projected statistical and work-load allocations. These are the actual outlays necessary to carry out the work of the service and must include all of the factors that influence costs. Table 4-2 shows one possible approach.

Again, it must be emphasized that the total FTE result reflects the established standard for any given time. The process identified here simply outlines their funding and the factors that influence their cost over the planned period.

The total number of hours worked for each FTE must be recorded and deducted from the total number of hours to be paid. This process determines the

Table 4-1 Format for Statistical Forecast

Nursing Department:___Oncology_____
Nurse Manager:___Jenifer Smith, R.N._____

Statistic:	Jan.	Feb.	Mar.	Apr.	May	June	July	Aug.	Sep.	Oct.	Nov.	Dec.	Total
Chemo	221	234	282	276	265	235	202	214	196	232	264	251	2,872
Immuno	83	76	89	82	79	90	67	70	72	86	91	68	953
Terminal –Care	13	12	14	15	13	12	11	10	12	14	15	11	152
_____													
_____													
_____													
_____													
_____													
_____													
_____													
_____													
_____													
_____													
Totals	317	322	385	373	357	337	280	294	280	332	370	330	3,977

Table 4-2 Human Resource Plan

Nursing Department:___Cardiac_____
Nurse Manager:___J. Jones, R.N._____
Total FTEs Planned:___16.4_____

Name		Smith 1.0	Jones 0.5	Mays 0.2
Worked Hours	+	1,880	940	396
Benefit Hours	+	180	90	16
Education Hours	+	20	10	4
Total Hours	=	2,080	1,040	416
Base $ Rate	×	9.45	9.28	9.56
Total $ Paid	=	19,656	9,651	3,977
Shift $ Differ.	+	–	–	396
Call $ Pay	+	96	–	–
Clinical $ Ladder	+	2,080	1,040	416
Overtime $ Amount	+	1,475	738	–
Other $	+	100	–	–
Total Paid Amount Planned	=	23,407	11,429	4,789
FICA Rate %	×	7.15	7.15	7.15
Total Budget Amount	=	25,081	12,246	5,131

total number of hours to be paid based on the hours needed. These include all the benefit hours provided as a component of employment. This information usually is computerized and can be calculated quickly and presented to the manager. As noted, the manager must know the origin of each statistic and calculation and how they affect her distribution of financial resources. All this will be helpful in keeping each component clear as she constructs her financial plan.

Each FTE's record is based on the total number of hours worked and how the manager has distributed them to meet her scheduling needs. The format in Table 4-2 allows the manager to identify the total number of worked hours by simply deducting the benefit and educational hours from the total hours paid for each FTE or portion of an FTE. Whatever the mechanism used by each institution, the worked hours must be identified separately for salary (payroll) purposes. This also shows the manager how much work time must be scheduled and how it should be distributed. Another factor that must be included is the hours worked by substitutes for vacations, holidays, and sick leave.

In Table 4-2, benefit time has been prorated to the percentage of an FTE. Since each institution usually has its own way of making its calculations, the manager must ascertain how it is done by her own facility.

PATIENT CLASSIFICATION AND PERSONNEL NEEDS

Influencing the development of a human resource budget, obviously, is the need for staff. Clearly, if there is no work, there is no need for staff. What is important is the relationship between the amount of work to be done and the number of appropriate people available to do it. This match is essential if the budget plan is to have meaning. Therefore, there must be a relationship between the statistic and the institution's FTE staffing standard. The question is: What is the appropriate standard for the statistic or what is the service requirement for each patient who makes use of the service? These questions underlie the development and use of most patient classification systems. (This text is not designed to undertake a detailed discussion of patient classification systems.)

The important point is the need for clear expression of the relationship between the work done and the needs of the client being served.

Staffing needs are closely tied to the patient classification system. These systems usually break down the care into identifiable elements to which time factors have been assigned. These time determinants collectively indicate the resources necessary to provide the required services. They also serve as a part of the standard for care against which all service can be evaluated. They can produce a predictor of the care needed so as to determine the personnel costs for the delivery of service.

An effective standards-based and replicable patient or service classification system is valuable in planning, forecasting, and evaluating services. The manager can predict the service requirements of a planning period by multiplying the service statistic (cases, patients, clients, etc.) by the standard (hours, service time needed), as identified in Chapter 3 (see Exhibit 4-1).

Each area of statistics must relate specifically to a defined service of the department; therefore, statistics must be developed for every service area. They should be linked to standards that relate to the work requirements. In this way the standard for workload determination matches as closely as possible the service being provided.

The nurse manager must focus on determining direct needs for all the services her unit offers, for two important reasons:

1. The manager must be able to determine appropriate work standards in order to assure that there is a direct relationship between her staffing levels and the work requirements of her service.
2. The manager must know the cost relationships in providing services before she can develop a charging structure.

In nursing, human resources constitute the largest cost items. Because of their size, they can have a dramatic impact on the financial viability of the

Exhibit 4-1 Statistic and Standard FTE Determination

Oncology Ambulatory Nursing Service												
Jan.	*Feb.*	*Mar.*	*Apr.*	*May*	*June*	*July*	*Aug.*	*Sep.*	*Oct.*	*Nov.*	*Dec.*	*Totals*
Statistic: Oncology Chemotherapy Visits												
221	234	282	276	265	235	202	214	196	232	264	251	2,872
Standard: Nursing Hours per Visit												
2.2	2.2	2.2	2.2	2.2	2.2	2.2	2.2	2.2	2.2	2.2	2.2	
Total Nursing Hours per Visit												
486	515	620	607	583	517	444	471	431	510	581	552	6,317
Total FTEs Required (2,080 X)												*Mean*
2.8	3.0	3.6	3.5	3.4	3.0	2.6	2.7	2.5	2.9	3.4	3.2	3.1
Distribution: All-R.N. Staff												
Work Time: 5-Day Week, 8-Hour Day												

Note: If the service requires a seven-day work week, the FTEs calculated must be spread over seven days. In the case of standards-based staffing, the standard always determines the number of FTEs required.

organization. The nurse manager thus must focus care and attention on the development of the data base that will support her financial plan.

All staffing plans and schedules are built on the data base for the projected services. If the service will operate more than the eight-hour standard day, that will have an impact on the time and salary calculations.

INSTITUTIONALLY SPONSORED EDUCATION TIME

Continuing professional development is a responsibility shared by the professional staff and the institution. The degrees of responsibility shared are specific to each facility. Each will have its own approach and allocations, depending on philosophy and management approach. The nurse manager must allocate her education dollars, if any, in a way acceptable to both the institution and her service. Many institutions still do not have a regularized mechanism for addressing this area from year to year. Some separate provision should be made to identify, allocate, and control costs related to both staff time and the expense of offering educational services.

In an era of decentralization, it is advisable to plan the educational expense within the same unit-based cost accounting framework as all other costs. Some institutions use a more centralized education department approach. This is not recommended, for two reasons: responsibility and control. If responsibility for continuing development is a major component of the professional role of the staff members, it is logical that they should be involved in a major way in its management. Education thus should be as close to the unit or department as possible. If the manager is responsible for controlling the resource use of her unit or department, she obviously must have a major role in its design. Allocating those costs at the unit level provides a better locus of control and use and a better opportunity to account for it.

The method of allocation depends totally on the needs of the institution and how it values education. Processes as complex as allocating permissible dollar or hour amounts per category of FTE or as simple as allotting a dollar amount per FTE are used by institutions that budget for education. However this process is evolved in a specific facility, some mechanism for accounting for staff education should be included in the financial plan.

If educational time is planned within the framework of worked time it must be deducted from the total amount of allocated time worked. This will raise some controversial issues. Many institutions do not feel that the individual should "replace" the time spent in educational activities by additional hours of work because she is away from patient care responsibilities. However, there is little rational argument to support this viewpoint.

It usually comes down to a matter of philosophy and commitment. If the health care facility regards education of its nursing staff as important to the delivery of standards-based service, then that commitment demands full support. To do less would be merely giving lip service to the commitment. The real message would become apparent when the resources to support the commitment were not forthcoming.

Patient care needs do not stop when the practitioners take educational courses. Commitment to education of caregivers is not a substitute for care; rather, it is an adjunct to it. Care continues. Educational activities do not change patients' needs, and nurses must be responsive to that reality regardless of any other consideration. It is just good business. The nurse manager must assure that the educational process is integrated into the plan and that the staffing variables influenced by the education component are addressed in the FTE allocation.

When these hours are totaled, they constitute the human resource hours data base for the budget plan. They are the total standard or regular hour determinations for each FTE for which dollar amounts will be determined. Multiplying each of these FTE base hour allocations by the base rate for each FTE will give the regular rate total dollar amounts to which will be added the other dollar considerations stemming from the characteristics of specific units.

DETERMINATION OF EDUCATION HOURS

Establishing standards for staff education time is an important function of a service or institution in providing an appropriate amount of care time for improving levels of competence and currency with clinical practice. In some areas, that educational time has been determined by the state; most, however, have not set such a standard so it is up to each facility to determine how it will best allocate educational time.

Unfortunately, many services do not provide for educational time in the work schedule; where it is incorporated in the work time, in which case both staff and patient care are short-changed. That may be one reason why many staff developers claim they receive inadequate response from the staff when the institution provides educational opportunities. Accurate resource allocation requires that the distribution of activities be assigned properly and accounted for to ensure that the controls necessary to measure budgetary performance are correct.

One reason that budget plans fail in the long term is the fact that the staff does not take advantage of the full range of activities for which funds have been provided—or that no funds have been provided. This ultimately affects both credibility and effectiveness. Education of nursing staff appears to be one of those areas affected by a process that often provides dollars but no time, or time but no dollars.

Perhaps the most effective way to allocate resources for education is to establish a consistent standard. That should define clearly the number of hours each staff member is expected to devote to education and should allocate the resources for attaining the standard. The department or service could define more specifically the educational content required, but for budgeting purposes a time standard pinpoints the dollar factors more accurately.

The simplest way to program educational dollars is to multiply the staff hour rate by the number of education hours allocated. This defines the specific cost for educational expectations (see Exhibit 4-2).

Requirements for other categories of personnel may vary, depending on the service or the need.

The allocation of educational time does not assure that it will be utilized. This is important because of the possibility that if it is not used, it may be lost to the service or department in the next budget negotiations. If educational time is established as a staff performance standard, a comparison of its use with its allocation may provide proof that it meets both criteria.

Exhibit 4-2 Determination of Education Hours

```
                Required Education Hours per Year per FTE: 18
                Number of FTEs Eligible for Education: 3.1
                Hourly Rate per FTE:
                        FTE 1.0 = $9.45
                        FTE 1.0 =  9.48
                        FTE 0.5 =  9.32
                        FTE 0.3 =  9.36
                        FTE 0.3 =  9.79
                Calculations:
                        1.0 FTE × 9.45 × 18 Hours = $170
                        1.0 FTE × 9.48 × 18 Hours =  171
                        0.5 FTE × 9.32 × 18 Hours =   84
                        0.3 FTE × 9.36 × 18 Hours =   51
                        0.3 FTE × 9.79 × 18 Hours =   53
                                            Total  $529
                Total Planned Education Hours Paid: 55.8
                Total Planned Education Dollars: $529
```

SHIFT DIFFERENTIALS

If a service requires work at times other than the normal five-day, Monday-Friday, eight-hour work period, some accommodation must be made in the financial plan. In most cases, shift differentials are a fixed dollar figure that is added to the amounts allocated for the FTE.

Health care institutions use many combinations of shift allocation and staff configurations. Shifts can range anywhere from the standard one turn five days a week, to three shifts seven days a week, to two 12-hour shifts, to weekends-only, to ten hours four days a week, etc. Such varying schedules clearly will have a dramatic impact on the allocation of shift differentials. They must be calculated consistent with the shift design.

If a 12-hour shift is offered for a seven-day-on, seven-day-off schedule, the calculation of routine time reflects an 84-hour work period in a single week. With allocations of eight hours a day, four hours are expended every day beyond the eight hours. Some may suggest that a differential should be paid in such circumstances. However, since this schedule is based on an 80-hour work period, the differential might not be justified.

There may be need for a differential for the most disadvantageous shift, usually the night shift, to encourage nurses to help fill the staffing needs of that period. Much of the rationale for shift differential is precisely to encourage staff to accept nondesirable hours of work for the additional financial benefit. Each institution must determine for itself what range of shift distributions will be acceptable and can be afforded. The amount of the shift differential also is a subjective consideration. Market conditions certainly would have some influence, but often the real decision must be based on what it takes to induce nurses to staff the shifts.

DETERMINATION OF SHIFT DIFFERENTIAL

If there are requirements for work beyond the normal work time, some mechanism usually is needed to compensate for the inconvenience and difficulty in finding and keeping personnel for those schedules.

The nurse manager must know first how much service will be provided in the time categories where shift differentials are needed. This can be interpreted most easily into the percentage of time needed when compared with all the available time. This percentage of service would have a direct impact on the amount of human resources that might be allocated to meet the work needs of that time. The manager also must consider the acuity indexes that might project the kinds of care that would be needed on the shift for which a differential is being considered. These determinations produce the work needs that must be factored into the financial plan.

Determination of the appropriate FTEs will follow the identification of the amount of time distributed over more than one shift. Since that time will be a percent of the whole, distribution of the FTE needs will match the percentage. Service hours required therefore must equal staff time provided. Exhibit 4-3 shows the determinations for two 12-hour shifts and three 8-hour shifts. The service workloads are determined to be different on the second shift (and third shift), presumably through a patient acuity system, so staff distribution on the second and third shifts is reduced.

In the first example, it is determined that a total of 18.5 FTEs are required to meet the twenty-four-hour needs of the service; 40 percent indicates that 7.4 FTEs are required on the second shift. In the second example, the personnel resources determined to be needed are, for the second shift, 30 percent of the daytime level, and for the third shift, 25 percent.

Management, nursing staff and the personnel department determined that the nursing differential amount in the first example would be $2, and in the second example, $1 for the second shift and $2 for the third shift. The differential amount applies only to time worked and thus is not considered in the benefits or any other calculations of salary.

Each institution should have its own guidelines and formulas for shift pay scales. Many institutions incorporate this process in the annual computerized budget program. The nurse manager must be aware of how the process operates and its impact on her service to assure that adequate resources have been allocated to meet the work demands.

Exhibit 4-3 Shift Differential Determination

Number of Shifts: 2
Total Number of FTEs: 18.5
Length of Worked Shift: 12 Hours
Worked Hours: 1,880
Shift Differential: $2.00 per Hour
Shift Staff Distribution:
   First Shift 60%
   Second Shift 40%
Calculation:
   40% × 18.5 × $2.00 = $14.80
   $14.80 × 1,880 = $27,824
Shift Differential Amount: $27,824

Number of Shifts: 3
Number of FTEs: 18.5
Length of Worked Shift: 8 Hours
Worked Hours: 1,880
Shift differential:
   Second Shift $1.00 per Hour
   Third Shift $2.00 per Hour
Distribution of Staff:
   First Shift 45%
   Second Shift 30%
   Third Shift 25%
Calculations:
   30% × 18.5 × $1.00 = $5.55
   $5.55 × 1,880 = $10,434
Second Shift Differential Amount: $10,434
Calculations:
   25% × 18.5 × $2.00 = $9.26
   $9.26 × 1,880 = $17,408
Third Shift Differential Amount: $17,408
Total Differential: $27,842

Determining the percentage of staff resources needed over any given time in all shifts indicates the FTE requirements and how they are "spread" over the whole day. In Exhibit 4-3, it was determined that there will be 45 FTEs on the first shift, 30 on the second, and 25 on the third. The same mathematical process is applied in this example. The variables applied here are the amount of staff that is appropriate, the percentage distribution of that staff, and the amount of differential allocated to that time and service. This example uses $1/hour for second shift and $2/hour for third shift. After the necessary resource use is determined, it is multiplied by the appropriate percentage and dollar amount per hour worked, and the total shift differential amount can be determined.

CLINICAL/CAREER LADDERS

A growing number of institutions have developed an in-house mechanism for rewarding nursing staff members for accomplishing certain goals judged to indicate their increased value to the service. Whether or not these programs are worthwhile or effective must be determined in terms of the values and results of each setting. The budget process must include a standard mechanism for providing appropriate resources to fund this program.

To determine bottom-line figures in structuring the expenditures for each cost center in this program, the manager must know how many persons will be needed, at what level, and at what time during the budget year. In many facilities, this figure is assigned as either a program cost or a divisional cost under its own heading. This does not reflect the degree of decentralization that appears to be shaping the financing of the future, but it does provide an efficient mechanism for allocating these costs. The recommended process is to assign these amounts to the budgets of each cost center.

In the allocation of call pay, it is recommended that the amounts not be included in the hourly rate but that they be added in the budget, outside of that calculation. The hourly rate should reflect the value of a position but should not take into account any personnel benefits.

As indicated in Table 4-2 earlier, each allocation should be posted in the month in which it occurs or as it is projected. For example, if a staff nurse is at Level 2 at the beginning of the budget year, that should appear in the first period or month. If the nurse has indicated a desire to reach Level 3, the amount for that level should be budgeted for the month in which she is expected to achieve it. Such a projection requires some planning on the part of the staff regarding their own career intentions and incorporating those staff plans into the fiscal plan for the service or the department.

OVERTIME

Probably no issue raises as much controversy as overtime. Not a few fiscal officers believe an effective organization should not plan for overtime. However, no one can plan so perfectly that all contingencies have been anticipated. There will be some disparity between the work time planned and the demand for a specific service. Planned overtime takes these factors into consideration.

Unfortunately there is no standard formula or amount that can be applied to the planning of overtime. Many figures have been suggested as appropriate for a budget—anywhere from 5 to 10 percent of the personnel worked dollars. No standard amount can or should apply to all institutions. Each service should look carefully at its characteristics and plan for the next year. From that, the manager must extrapolate a standard that is expected to meet the needs of the service. Overtime never should be used as an excuse for poor projection and planning. The "just-in-case" approach gives the process a negative character and impairs trust in the institution's planning process.

The best method for planning overtime is to spread a flat amount per month over the year. The process also should make provision for overtime on shifts other than daytime, factoring in shift differentials. If the health care institution has a union contract, that document must be considered. If possible, the overtime should be broken down by amount per type of individual staff member.

Some institutions use a process allowing department managers broader budget control. While this may seem overly detailed, most managers will have assistance from computers. In fact, much of such detailed computations already have been done by computers, leaving the manager the responsibility of providing the final inputs, verifying the computer output, and monitoring the results.

Exhibit 4-4 offers one way to address the calculation of overtime. This calls for a multiplication of 1.5 times the hourly rate for every hour of overtime. Of course, it is a good management strategy to spread the use of overtime equally among staff members.

OTHER HUMAN RESOURCE ITEMS

The institution also has other human resources expenses. In most facilities, these are included in the benefits allocations and are determined as a percentage

Exhibit 4-4 Projection of Overtime Hours

Calculated by Percent of Total FTE Hours
Historical Data: Overtime percent during last two fiscal
planning periods = 5%
Total FTEs: 3.1
Calculation of Overtime Hours:
FTE 1.0 = 1,880 (hours worked) × 5% OT = 94 OT Hours
FTE 1.0 = 1,880 (hours worked) × 5% OT = 94 OT Hours
FTE 0.5 =   940 (hours worked) × 5% OT = 47 OT Hours
FTE 0.3 =   564 (hours worked) × 5% OT = 28 OT Hours
FTE 0.3 =   564 (hours worked) × 5% OT = 28 OT Hours

Total Overtime Hours = 291

Calculation of Overtime Dollars:
94 OT Hours (1.0 FTE) × $9.45 × 1.5 = $1,332
94 OT Hours (1.0 FTE) × $9.48 × 1.5 = 1,337
47 OT Hours (0.5 FTE) × $9.32 × 1.5 =   657
28 OT Hours (0.5 FTE) × $9.79 × 1.5 =   411
28 OT Hours (0.5 FTE) × $9.36 × 1.5 =   393

Total Overtime Dollars = 4,130

of total salary and wages. Such items as health insurance, life insurance, retirement plans, bonuses, and tuition payments all are in this special category. This area, too, is unique to each institution, with varying amounts and contributions to these programs. The nurse manager must have a clear idea of these special benefits in her institution and how they are applied to each employee. These are included in the computer calculation for each employee based on such factors as length of service, role, and employment status (full-time or part-time). Not to be overlooked are local, state, and federal tax allocations.

In a separate benefits allocation are the dollars set aside for Workers' Compensation claims. This benefit covers employees' accidents or disease from work-related activities. It usually is included in the overall calculation of benefits but seldom is done individually in the service or department; in fact, in most facilities it is handled by the personnel office and is a part of its budget plan.

When all of these factors are totaled per individual staff member in each category and summed, a picture is created laterally by category of item and vertically by employee total. This enables the nurse manager to analyze the item amounts both individually and collectively by a graph. When multiplied by the FICA (Social Security tax), the total for each employee can be identified, and the total for all is obtained when added laterally across all staff members for all personnel-related costs.

CALL PAY

The calculation of call pay should be based strictly on projected use and validated by historical data. It should reflect program requirements and relate specifically to the function for which it is being provided. Of the many reasons for using call pay, most relate to the provision of service at times other than regularly scheduled work periods, requiring the availability of skilled personnel.

Decisions on the appropriateness of call pay are specific to each institution. Some may have a wide need, others may make little use of it—all influenced by the facility's requirements and its philosophy of time and pay allocations.

Calculation of call pay depends on the amount of dollars per hour allocated multiplied by the number of call hours projected. The variable in this calculation is the category of person and the call amount attached to that category (see Exhibit 4-5).

While call pay provides a flexible approach, it also can be abused easily. When services are required, call pay can be one of the most efficient mechanisms for paying for the care while keeping overall service costs to a minimum. However, there is a temptation to increase the number of services for which a need for call pay is presumed to exist. Approval of call pay should be based on analysis of the service and its personnel needs and balancing that against the benefits.

Exhibit 4-5 Determination of Call Pay

Number of Call Hours Required per Year:
Number of Call Hours × Number of Days On Call = Number of Call Hours
Example:
   16 Call Hours per day
   × 260 Call Days per Year
   = 4,160 Call Hours per Year
   Call Rate Paid per Call Hour: $2
   Annual Cost for Call Time: $8,320

Call per Person Calculated as a Factor of FTE
   Number of FTEs: 3.1
   Number of Call Hours Allocated: 4,160
   4,160 (Total Call Hours) ÷ 3.1 FTEs = 1342 Call Hours per FTE
   Distribution of Call Hours per Year among the FTEs:
     1.0 FTE = 1,342
     1.0 FTE = 1,342
     0.5 FTE =   671[a]
     0.3 FTE =   403[b]
     0.3 FTE =   403[c]
     Total   = 4,161

a. 0.5 FTE × 1,342 Call Hours = 671 Call Hours per Year
b. 0.3 FTE × 1,342 Call Hours = 403 Call Hours per Year
c. 0.3 FTE × 1,342 Call Hours = 403 Call Hours per Year

RECRUITMENT, HIRING, AND TURNOVER COSTS

Needless to say, human resource management includes the need to control the costs associated with change. Nothing remains the same. People come and go in any work setting. This reality must be built into the operation of any service.

Recruitment

A key part of the nurse manager's role is assuring that the right person is in the right job at the right time. Most facilities include nursing recruitment in the service's budget. In decentralized organizations, much of these costs are allocated to individual services. As nurse shortages become the norm rather than the unexpected, the need for effective recruitment will be more important. Larger facilities will set aside funds for the full range of recruitment and its support elements. Budgeting for this service has the same characteristics as any other program function. All program-related costs must be built into the recruitment budget and projected over the planning period. Costs usually associated with recruitment include:

- nurse recruiter
- marketing services and supplies
- benefits allocations
- office space and services
- telephone and other utilities
- publication and material support, etc.

Recruitment costs usually are contingent upon the changes anticipated in personnel. It is not always clear at budget time what changes will occur in the next year (or other time span). The nurse manager can predict change, but, given the varieties and problems of humankind, not always accurately. In such circumstances, the nurse manager must rely on historical data and on her relationship with her staff. Each will provide as accurate a predictor as is possible.

Hiring and Orientation

A significant and often hidden cost involves the hiring and orienting of new staff members. For example, the cost of staff time in bringing the new member to full participation in the unit program can be considerable. These are often the forgotten costs yet they must be accounted for.

The orientation program should be standardized to the specific needs of the department or service. The time and depth of the orientation should be clearly established, described, and accounted for. While each orientee may generate costs for certain individualized needs, there should be enough historical data on overall time and personnel costs that the nurse manager can make a reasonably accurate budget projection.

Other common hiring costs include relocation expenses, where paid. This usually has been reserved primarily for clinical personnel or top management. Special benefits often are made available as inducements to particularly desired new persons; these, too, add to the cost of recruitment and must be contained to the extent possible. If they are continuing benefits, they must appear in the staff budget (Table 4-2).

Turnover

Once people are hired, there is no guarantee how long they will stay. Statistics that identify the historical turnover experience can be a valuable aid for the nurse manager in assessing the probable impact of turnover within a given budget period. Collection of such data is easy. Their basic value is in providing the monthly and annual turnover rates. These are obtained by calculating the percent of staff resignations or terminations in a defined period as a portion of the staff allocated—dividing the number of turnovers by the number of approved staff positions. Hours worked in any given period also can be used to calculate turnover for that span by translating the positions into hours, then dividing the hours by the total number of approved work hours in the period.

For example, in one month, 173 hours usually are expended in a full-time position. If the unit lost one full-time position out of 20 at the beginning of the work period (173 $\times$ 20 = 3,460), that sum is divided into the hours of the vacated position (173 $\div$ 3,460 = 0.05) giving a 5 percent turnover rate for the month.

Turnover statistics are important to management. They provide a clear indication of the status of the nurse manager's staffing situation. High turnover can be an indicator of external or internal stressors affecting her service. Turnover can give some indication of the success of her style of management and her leadership skills. It also can identify problems or situations that are unanticipated but for which a management response is indicated.

SUMMARY

The human resource budget is multifaceted. Many considerations must be incorporated into the process of planning the providing of such resources. This function is central to the provision of all nursing services. In this case, the adage that people are the greatest asset holds true. Because this is especially true in nursing, it is vital that good planning be a basis for the allocation of those resources and the financing necessary to support them.

A systematic and thorough approach to the budget planning process is essential in human resources management. The use of historical and projection data, and the building of operating and control systems, will provide the essential tools for managing the fiscal plan for personnel. It is important also not to overlook such essential factors as overtime, education, recruitment, and orientation costs. Attention to the detail of financing for the human resource at this planning stage will save the nurse manager much time, grief, adjustment, or retrenchment later in the budget year.

SUGGESTED READINGS

Clark, R.C. "Does the Nonprofit Form Fit the Hospital Industry?" *Harvard Law Review* (May 1980):1417–89.

Hoffman, Francis M. *Financial Management for Nurse Managers*. Norwalk, Conn. Appleton-Century-Crofts, 1984, 73–117.

Lohman, R.A. *Breaking Even: Financial Management In Human Service Organizations*. Philadelphia: Temple University Press, 1980.

Appendix 4-A

Exercise and Practice Tools

Exercise 4-1 Statistical Forecast

Nursing Department: _____

Nurse Manager: _____

Statistic:	Jan.	Feb.	Mar.	Apr.	May	June	July	Aug.	Sep.	Oct.	Nov.	Dec.	Total
Totals													

Exercise 4-2 Human Resource Plan

Nursing Department:_____
Nurse Manager:_____
Total FTEs Planned:_____

Name													
Worked Hours	+												
Benefit Hours	+												
Education Hours	+												
Total Hours	=												
Base $ Rate	×												
Total $ Paid	=												
Shift $ Differ.	+												
Call $ Pay	+												
Clinical $ Ladder	+												
Overtime $ Amount	+												
Other $	+												
Total Paid Amount Planned	=												
FICA Rate	×												
Total Budget Amount	=												

Exercise 4-3 Statistic and Standard FTE Determination

Nursing Service
Statistic: Visits, Patient Days, etc.

Jan.	Feb.	Mar.	Apr.	May	June	July	Aug.	Sep.	Oct.	Nov.	Dec.	Totals

Standard: Nursing Hours per Visit

Total Nursing Hours per Visit

Total FTEs Required (2,080 X)   *Mean*

Distribution: _____

Work Time: _____

Note: If the service requires a seven-day workweek, the FTEs calculated must be spread over seven days. In the case of standards-based staffing, the standard always determines the number of FTEs required.

Exercise 4-4 Shift Differential Determination

Number of Shifts: _____
Total Number of FTEs: _____
Length of Worked Shift: _____Hours
Worked Hours: _____
Shift Differential: $_____ per Hour
Shift Staff Distribution:
   First Shift _____%
   Second Shift _____%
Calculation:
   _____% × _____ × $_____ =

   $_____ × 1,880 =
Shift Differential Amount: $_____

Number of Shifts: _____
Number of FTEs: _____
Length of Worked Shift: _____Hours
Worked Hours: _____
Distribution of Staff:
   First Shift _____%
   Second Shift _____%
   Third Shift _____%
Shift Differential:
   Second Shift $_____ per Hour
   Third Shift $_____ per Hour
Calculations:
   _____% × _____ × $_____ =

   $_____ × 1,880 =
Second Shift Differential Amount: _____
Calculations:
   _____% × _____ × $_____ =

   $_____ × _____ =
Third Shift Differential Amount: _____
Total Differential: _____

Exercise 4-5 Determination of Education Hours

Required Education Hours per Year per FTE: _____
Number of FTEs Eligible for Education: _____
Hourly Rate per FTE:

   FTE _____ = $_____
   FTE _____ = $_____
   FTE _____ = $_____
   FTE _____ = $_____
   FTE _____ = $_____

Calculations:

_____FTE × $_____ × _____Hours = $_____
_____FTE × $_____ × _____Hours = $_____
_____FTE × $_____ × _____Hours = $_____
                                    Total   _____

Total Planned Education Hours Paid: _____

Total Planned Education Dollars: $_____

Exercise 4-6 Projection of Overtime Hours

Calculated by Percent of Total FTE Hours

Historical Data: Overtime percent during last two fiscal planning
            periods = _____

Total FTEs: _____

Calculation of Overtime Hours:

FTE _____ = _____(hours worked) × _____% OT = _____OT Hours

FTE _____ = _____(hours worked) × _____% OT = _____OT Hours

FTE _____ = _____(hours worked) × _____% OT = _____OT Hours

FTE _____ = _____(hours worked) × _____% OT = _____OT Hours

FTE _____ = _____(hours worked) × _____% OT = _____OT Hours

                  Total Overtime Hours = _____

Calculation of Overtime Dollars:

_____OT Hours (_____ FTE) × $_____ × 1.5 = $_____

_____OT Hours (_____ FTE) × $_____ × 1.5 = $_____

_____OT Hours (_____ FTE) × $_____ × 1.5 = $_____

_____OT Hours (_____ FTE) × $_____ × 1.5 = $_____

_____OT Hours (_____ FTE) × $_____ × 1.5 = $_____

            Total Overtime Dollars = $_____

Exercise 4-7 Determination of Call Pay

Number of Call Hours Required per Year:

Number of Call Hours × Number of Days On Call = Number of Call Hours

> Example:
>   16 Call Hours per day
>   × 260 Call Days per Year
>   = 4,160 Call Hours per Year
>   Call Rate Paid per Call Hour: $2
>   Annual Cost for Call Time: $8,320

Call per Person Calculated as a Factor of FTE

Number of FTEs: _____

Number of Call Hours Allocated: _____

_____ (Total Call Hours) ÷ _____FTEs = _____Call Hours per FTE

Distribution among the FTEs:

_____ FTE _____Call Hours per Year

_____ FTE _____Call Hours per Year

_____ FTE _____Call Hours per Year

_____ FTE _____Call Hours per Year

_____ FTE _____Call Hours per Year

Total _____Call Hours

The Cost of Nursing Care

OBJECTIVES FOR CHAPTER 5

This chapter will:
1. *Discuss the necessity for and the essential components of quantifying nursing care.*
2. *Identify specific characteristics of the establishment of an acuity-based nursing care delivery system.*
3. *Identify the specific factors affecting patient acuity processes.*
4. *Explore basic components and processes of building a patient accounting framework.*
5. *Review the data characteristics and utilization of data in the context of patient care accounts.*
6. *Outline the specific historical data essential to building the nursing unit or departmental budget.*
7. *Review four important aspects of the human resource system in the use of objective and acuity-related data.*

The manager must consider many components of nursing in planning for the resource costs of offering a service. In the late 1980s, the demand was greater than ever for an integrated account-based approach to the costing and valuing of nursing services. In an age marked by dwindling resources, there is a need to (1) develop systems that track as well as determine the appropriateness of service costs in offering essential services and (2) integrate systems that not only define the parameters for viable services but also account for their cost and value to patients.

The nurse manager must have a mechanism for integrating the cost and components of nursing and creating a system for accounting and controlling that relationship (see Exhibit 5-1).

Exhibit 5-1 Quantifying Nursing Care

Establishing a Nursing Care Standard:
- Study Work Process
- Establish Time Parameters
- Accept Defined Time Standards
- Define Nursing Categories
- Develop Nursing Operating System
- Integrate with Finance Framework
- Certify Care/Cost Framework

The planning process must have tools that systematically quantify nursing care. There must be a direct and manageable relationship between describing nursing care and attaching a monetary value to it. To assure reliability, all the functional processes must be replicable. The nurse manager must be reminded of her fundamental obligations to both her nursing peers and the consumer of care. Because of the structure of the health care system and the focus on controlling costs, the manager must be aware at all times that she must tie service (nursing care) to cost (paying for care). While this is an elementary point, implementing strategies and processes that evidence this in daily practice is difficult. The successful manager will apply political, social, and economic variables to the planning process and to decisions she makes with regard to nursing services, resource use, and consumer satisfaction (see Figure 5-1).

It is not the intent here to undertake an exhaustive discussion regarding the development of patient classification or cost systems for nursing. Obviously, the components of such systems must be in place to account for and control the resources needed to provide care in an efficient and economic manner. This chapter discusses the essential elements that must be in place if the manager is to have an effective control process. Specific approaches to managing this process must be left to readers in their own settings.

ACUITY INDEXES

For finance purposes, acuity indexes have an entirely different value for the nurse manager than for the clinical manager. Acuity indexes provide a baseline of information regarding severity of illness or intensity of nursing care that is essential in building a patient-based valuing system. They generate information the manager needs to establish the cost parameters for services in both staffing and patient care. This baseline gives the manager an idea of total direct costs for each activity that is a part of providing services. Out of this, the manager can analyze the kind of nursing services she offers and the compatibility of those services with

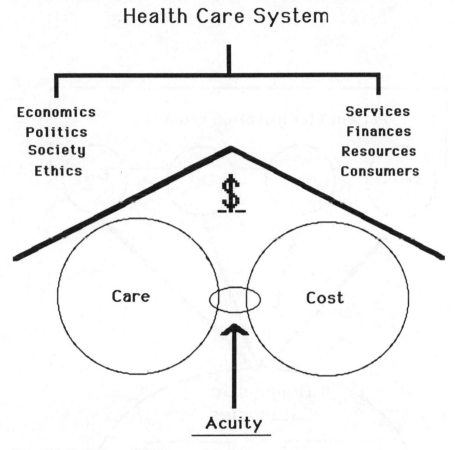

Health Care System

Economics	Services
Politics	Finances
Society	Resources
Ethics	Consumers

Figure 5-1 The Business of Nursing

the price paid for it as well as the extent and intensity of utilization of nursing services (see Figure 5-2).

When acuity is tied closely to a payment category such as a diagnosis related group (DRG), the cost of the nursing activity is added to other expenses in that category to obtain the total cost of that service. The manager can determine the nursing portion's percent of the total expense and its appropriateness in comparison with the total cost. A pricing structure then can be planned that reflects the service characteristics. Costs can be incorporated into the business plan for both the marketing and provision of services.

The new development in nursing budgeting is the accounts-based system. In this method, each patient and care category has cost and price parameters of its own that must be incorporated into the planning system. Each patient falls within

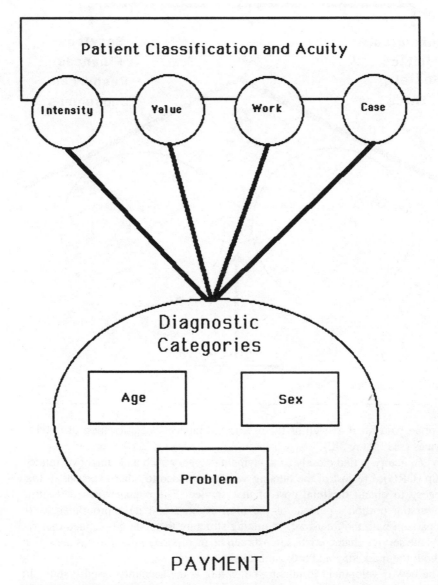

Figure 5-2 Patient Classification and Payment Integration

a defined set of care and financial characteristics that indicates the kind and intensity of nursing care needed. Individual variations must be scrutinized carefully to determine whether they indicate a pattern that can affect the service.

The organization of the costing framework is as important to the nurse manager as any of the components. It must have a statistical rationale. Nursing care components must be logical and easily interpretable. The classification of patient financial status and care must be associated with the clinical situation. This involves quantifying the nursing activity that will be needed. The categories of care then must fit within the larger diagnosis related group (DRG). This relationship remains constant, whatever the prevailing payment structure. DRGs will undoubtedly change into a more complex classification of services and payment structures. The nurse manager will be called upon to fit the nursing service needs into the appropriate payment system.

Acuity indicators must be quantitative, patient-specific indicators of the use of nursing resources. Included among processes that aim at obtaining solid indications of resources used are: staffing data, systems approach to nursing care delivery, nursing process and standards framework, evidence of kind and quality of care, and the appropriateness of the nursing management information system (see Figure 5-3). Quality control also must be an integral part of the system. Nurse managers must be concerned with the intensity (and thus cost) issues as well as with the clinical process.

The data generation process must be so structured as to produce meaningful information that in turn is easily transferable to the financial format to show the costs associated with providing care.

Since there is a direct relationship between the care given, its cost, and its value to both the patient and third party payer, there should be some measurable outcome to support the reasonableness of expending the dollars. It is important also to avoid to the extent possible, programs, services, or care that do not justify the spending or even produce losses.

The budget plan must include the standards for care that reflect the amount of staff needed for each type of patient service. Staff costs then are tied specifically to individual patients.

Projected staffing standards do not necessarily need to be static or fixed. Staffing will be based on the intensity of patient needs. For example, a patient just after surgery needs a greater mix or intensity of nursing care than one preparing for discharge. Except when the patient dies, the level of care intensity generally decreases fairly rapidly, reducing staff needs. The key intensity indicators are shown in Figure 5-4.

Severity of illness categories, as of the late 1980s, had not yet been integrated well with patient DRGs. The DRGs did not account adequately for the differences in severity of illness within the same category. For example, a patient may share a DRG class with another yet have an entirely different response to the illness

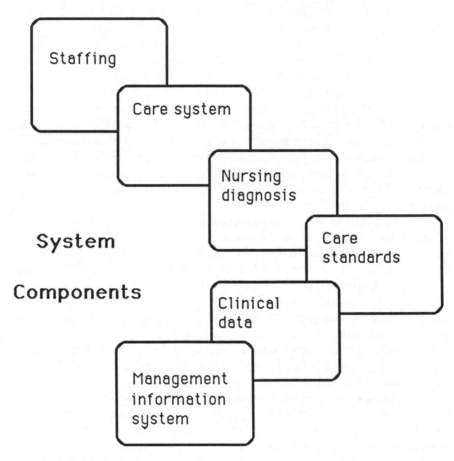

Figure 5-3 Patient Acuity System Factors

demanding either more or less resource use. Developing and using a good acuity system that effectively measures all the variables involving illness will provide the information necessary to make appropriate staff and care assignments and cost allocations.

In settings with a number of caregiver categories (licensed practical nurse, registered nurse, nursing assistant, and so on), it is necessary to allocate functional responsibilities and costs by nursing complexity of care or a process yet to be described by the nursing profession. Since the consumer or payer will be charged directly for the services rendered, there should be a mechanism to allocate the cost of delivering that service by category of care giver. This can be incorporated into the nursing care standard and calculated as a product of the intensity measure.

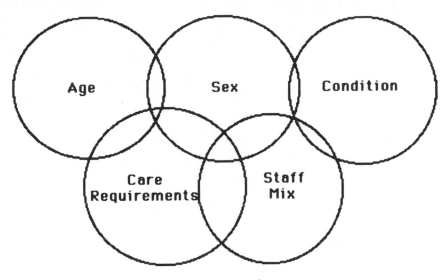

Figure 5-4 Intensity Indicators

Whatever the strategy for incorporating categories of care giver, the manager must be able to determine the overall cost of service and to allocate the expense of its elements to each person on the staff who provides the care. If there is a poor relationship between the cost and the care rendered through a poor match between staff cost and payment, the budget and the financial plan can be affected negatively.

BUILDING INDIVIDUAL ACCOUNTS

A care classification and costing process provides for assimilating the data into an accounts system. For purposes of simplicity, every patient is an account in the service delivery system. That account should contain all the cost items as well as income (payments) (Figure 5-5). When expenses are subtracted from the income, a positive balance should remain.

Naturally, all patients with similar illnesses should be put in the same categories of accounts. If, for example, one account category is broken hips, all patients in the institution with broken hips should be listed in that account category. The data from one patient in that category should be compared with the aggregate of all patients in that type of account. If the costs for any patient vary significantly from the norm, the nurse manager should review the care process. If on the other hand the care provided varies from the amount allotted as the price for a category, the care, diagnostic, support, therapeutic, and resource use items must be reviewed.

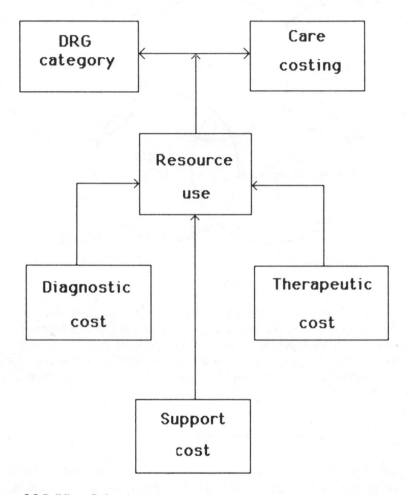

Figure 5-5 Building a Patient Account

A highly integrated approach to the management of nursing resource budgets and their operational components is essential. It should be clear that a basic understanding of both data base management and computer systems is necessary if the nurse executive is to manage highly sophisticated information complexes. It is through the coordination and integration of data that the manager creates an effective planning and monitoring system that enables her to control her resources. Since response time is vital in making rapid adjustments as needed in services and resources, her ability to obtain, review, and understand the data can make the difference between success and failure in a program or a system.

BUDGET PLANNING

The collection and use of data is an important portion of the budgeting process. Chapters 1 and 2 discussed the components of that function. The factors outlined there hold true for all data processes. The data generated by the clinical and cost system should produce information that will constitute the basis of the planning process and have a direct impact on the statistical elements used to plan responses to service needs.

The elements used in the human resource budget directly reflect the clinical data in the service and care categories. The calculations of worked time, overtime, call time, etc., depend on the need for services and their cost. Strategies for personnel utilization are determined in part by the comparison of current data with historical performance information. Each succeeding set of data helps fine-tune the framework for subsequent performance expectations.

The statistical data similarly form the basis for building each succeeding period's financial plan. The information that a nurse manager collects that relates specifically to patient care planning can make a difference when budgeting the next planning period.

All financial planning obviously depends in part on the quality of the historical data base. Historical data are important in determining the total dollars needed to operate the nursing service. The nurse executive competes with other managers in the institution for a stated amount of total resources. The ability to validate the necessary financing on the basis of a solid performance history can make a difference. The following factors are essential to her presentation.

Accurate Acuity Data

As indicated earlier, acuity data play a central role in validating the care and service needs of the patient population served. These data must be credible, easily understood, and well integrated with all other needed information. The data should be designed to assure that they apply specifically to the service.

"Canned" and preprogrammed approaches that cannot reflect the unique characteristics of a service are of limited value. The acuity characteristics must be easily transferrable to financial cost data. The ability to use these data both prospectively and retrospectively also is essential.

Nursing Standards of Care

Much has been written regarding the necessity for nursing care standards. In the data base for planning and costing, nursing care standards take on special meaning. These standards define the process and the actions appropriate for each specific type of care.

The acuity indexes must fit easily within the standards format, which structures the approach to the delivery of services as well as its cost. Care cannot be evaluated if the framework of standards is absent.

Patient/Client Statistical Data

The nursing management information system is an essential component in the collection and integration of meaningful data on nursing and its relation to other elements of care delivery.

Census, lengths of stay, patient days, costs per day, staffing, resource use, DRG classification, overhead costs, management and clerical costs, etc., all are valuable components of the data base. They can help make a difference in the effectiveness and efficiency of the manager's operation.

Financial/Clinical Integration

Vital to the successful management of the nursing service is a systematic integration of the financial components of the planning and operational processes. Costing and charging directly for services is standard business strategy. Nurse managers must be able to respond when strategies are not working in conjunction with each other and when the operating processes are at variance with the planning process.

When acuity, standards, care, and cost work in the planned manner, the manager's task is eased. The tying of all these pieces to a broad patient or client categorization such as the DRG system gives the manager an umbrella under which to address and evaluate all service components and their accounts. The viability of this integration helps determine the institution's successes and failures.

Institutional Viability

Nursing sometimes tends to forget that it is a part of a broader system whose components are integrated to support the institution's clinical, data, and financial management processes. The viability of the nursing system in relation to the institution's finance and data generation processes is important to both nursing and the facility as a whole.

Since payment systems have become more clinically specific, the nursing data and care system aid the institution in building and using a solid management and clinical data bank. Incorporation of the institution's leadership persons in planning and developing nursing's care/cost/charge system can assist in assuring its success and strengthen its operation and credibility. Integrating all of the institution's data reporting systems can be helpful to managers in their decision making.

Management Response

The ability to react to changes or variations in the data or operations in the care delivery system is central to good management control. Administration must make certain that all managers, including nursing, can access and respond to data. This response flexibility depends on the kind and quality of information available.

There certainly can be no closely held or unavailable information if it is pertinent and in some way has an impact on the nurse manager's planning and operating capability. The manager in turn must use the information appropriately in the department's control and monitoring processes. She must communicate all relevant information to the staff. Staff members must understand, and be encouraged to participate fully in, the data generation and analysis processes.

Here again, there can be no secrets. The direct relationship between the work roles and the service needs of the organization demands that all involved participate in its operation and in assuring appropriate response to any changes. Where a response cannot alter a situation, that fact must be included in the strategy. When planned strategies have been unsuccessful, they, too, must be confronted and appropriate adjustments made. Data and operating systems have little value if they do not stimulate appropriate action and responses.

SYSTEMS STEPS FOR DETERMINING CARE COSTS

It is not appropriate here to discuss a particular costing system or a process for integrating patient acuity and costing factors. Much software available in the marketplace does that adequately for a broad range of clinical nursing services. The last word has not been said about approaches or strategies on acuity/costing systems; the process remains dynamic. However, there are important aspects of such systems that must be in place if they are to have the desired impact on the financial processes in the division of nursing (see Exhibit 5-2).

Exhibit 5-2 Costing the Care

Engineered Standards
   Objectives
   Work Related
   Clinical Standards Based
   Evaluated Against Outcomes
Resources
   Mix of Staff
   Quality of Service
   Education Differentiation
   Service Requirements
Management Information Systems
   Valid Data
   Integrative Information
   Useful Data
   Decision Analysis
   Variance Reporting
   Planning Response

Engineered Standards

The standards of performance must have some rationale and must be justifiable and dependable. The system should reflect clearly the work characteristics that must be statistically and objectively measured to determine the supply of human resources to meet service requirements. This standard must be replicable and capable of evaluation and adjustment as indicated by the data analysis and variance reports. Nursing industrial engineers are usually utilized to obtain and generate the data base on which subsequent work standards will be founded.

Reasonable Resources

Perhaps less discussed yet vitally important to the quality of services is the mix of staff available for nursing care. The appropriate assignment of nursing resources is an important consideration in the delivery of those services.

While the mix of services must be validated, it is equally important to assure that those being offered are the best that can be obtained for the available resources. In the budgeting of human resources, the relationship between who offers those services and the quality of the care often does not receive adequate attention.

Staff Commitment

The value and accuracy of acuity and cost data are key elements necessary for the correlation of information upon which decisions will be made.

If there is an area where such information systems break down, it probably involves the lack of staff commitment and subsequent followthrough with data collection. In the development of the acuity/costing system it is vital to assure that members are fully involved in the process, as in any program of importance. They, as well as patients, are the beneficiaries and users of the service components developed with the help of the system.

Management Information System

There is little value in having effective measurement systems if they cannot tell managers what they need to know. Data must come together and present a result (a printout, for example) if they are to have any value. All too often, managers collect reams of data, little of which has any value other than to give them the opportunity to say they have it. Data must show something specific involving the action or operation of the organization to be of value. Collecting data for collection's sake—"just in case"—generally is a waste of time.

Data must inform the manager of the effectiveness and viability of the services. The information system should have components that address nursing service factors such as acuity, census, demographics, service, staffing, expenses, revenue, variances, etc.

Much of the information also should have broad application to the data in the rest of the institution and, when correlated with such material, give administration an analysis of the facility's progress and viability in terms of its goals and plans. Nursing data must be integrated with those of the other clinical services to give the institution some sense of the direction it should take.

While this may appear logical, the problem is that much of the data of the various services cannot be generalized to the entire institutional system. As a result, the organization never benefits fully. Indeed, managers may even make decisions that they never would have if they had had appropriate data available. This point has serious implications for institutions whose success depends in part on their ability to integrate systems and the data that support them.

This problem can be eased if the institution's management staff members undertake planning and discussions as to the kind of data required by all the services. In this way much of the ineffective, unnecessary, or relatively useless data would not be generated, saving time and energy. Improved data can produce more positive outcomes. Because the manager often does not know what to do with some of the data available, the originating department can provide advice on their proper use.

PLANNING AND OPERATING

One of the greatest areas of concern that often goes unaddressed in books of this kind is the importance and value of the relationship between the financial planning and operating processes. If there is a need for good relationships, it is in the finance system of the institution. The nurse manager needs the support of, and connectedness with, her peers both within and outside of her service. Some managers and the finance department lack mutual understanding and communication; neither can operate without the other, yet they often act like enemies in open warfare.

Whatever the reasons, in today's health care environment there is no room for division between clinical and financial services. If anything, there is a stronger need for their interaction because of the demands of the payment system. Financial data generated from the billing process and from the medical records system need to be melded with the data from the clinical services, including nursing, to provide a complete record of the patient's financial and care experience. Correlation of that information with other data from similar patients provides an overview of the institution's performance in a specified category of care.

Since accounts information is the central component of a good health services business, the more appropriate the data related to the management of the patient, the better the job of operating the service. To the extent that the data are lacking in specifics or in integration with the institution, quality and effectiveness are affected.

Costing obviously is related directly to the kind and quality of the data. Management must be able to generate and use meaningful data. In fact, the entire costing approach is dependent in large part on the management and clinical information available. The planning process, which is inextricably connected to data processes, will be measurably affected by the kind and quality of the information.

No plan can hope to be complete or viable if the manager does not have the quality and kind of information upon which to make critical decisions. Staffing levels, material and supply items, resource use, income generation, statistical and demographic patterns, and more—all are elements of the system that supports the costing of nursing services. They also indicate variations in plans and expectations and the kinds of responses the manager must make to assure adjustments and corrective actions are implemented when necessary.

An effective costing system relies heavily on the quality of the nursing information system. The nurse manager as business woman would be well advised to pay close attention to her data system. In it are the keys that unlock her responses to her daily operation and its variables.

She will find that reviewing the many approaches to nurse costing and the computerized systems will help her improve her effectiveness, particularly if she incorporates into her service some of the major data bases she will need to manage it. Such a cost accounting can benefit her directly and the data generated can help her avoid pitfalls that could prove financially disastrous for her service.

Effectiveness includes always being prepared for the eventualities of life. Without the right tools, such readiness can be impossible in the ever-changing world of health care services. The manager with the right data can respond quickly and effectively and can move ahead of others who may be struggling with the kind and quality of their materials. Good internal data and a solid fit with those generated elsewhere involving factors important to the nurse manager always will be advantageous.

The key is to have believable data and depend on them to give direction. Success is the ability of the manager to act quickly and know that the outcome will be what she anticipated and can be replicated on any number of occasions or in many circumstances.

ENGINEERED APPROACHES

The development of an appropriate patient classification system should be based on an objective approach. There are essential characteristics of such a system that are important in establishing a base for the development of a patient data monitoring mechanism. Patient classification should relate not only to the level of staffing but also to the impact of acuity on the processes of delivering nursing care.

All patient classification systems must meet some basic criteria:

- They must identify patients in conjunction with each other so that they can be classified into relatively clear categories of care.
- There must be a systematic and organized approach to the classification and integration of various patient types and components.
- The timing of each classification must be identified so that the numbers of classifications and the time it takes to deliver care can be consistent with the service offered.
- The calculation must make provision for the utilization of human resources and their application to the requirements for patient care.

There are almost as many patient classification systems available as there are institutions using them. The elements listed should be consistent within almost any such system. Two important questions are:

1. Has the patient classification approach been based on the real service provided?
2. Has it been determined objectively through an analysis of nursing work and the assessment of that work consistent with certain values or standards that indicate acceptable performance levels in relation to care delivery?

The issue of acceptable nursing care often is relatively unaddressed. Task, work flow, chart, and/or time and motion analysis may serve as the sole basis for determining classifications. One of the greatest failures of most systems is that they do not address adequately some of the real-time variables that affect the utilization of the persons who deliver the nursing care being assessed.

In establishing standards, the relationship between patient and nurse may not reflect on cost and resource availability. As a result, systems in many institutions indicate that they need more resources than they have available. This causes management and staff members to doubt the viability and validity of their patient classification system, to look at it with a jaundiced eye, and to fail to use it appropriately.

The nurse manager must be careful to conduct a balanced and systematic assessment of the variables that go into the design of the classification system. She always should keep in mind her ability to respond to the following questions:

1. Am I using objective processes to determine the relationship between nursing staffing needs and patient acuity levels?
2. What is the financial framework within which I operate that provides the resources for nursing care and how flexible is it in responding to changes in acuity?
3. What do acuity and patient classification measures indicate when correlated with financial, standards, and quality indexes that define the nursing care expectations on an individual unit, department, or service?
4. How deeply is the nursing staff involved in the process of classifying and utilizing the data for determining patient care needs and staffing levels?
5. Does the patient classification system serve as a component of the data base that assists the manager in making decisions on allocation and utilization of human resources for delivering standard-based nursing care, meeting the predefined levels of quality, and operating within the prescribed financial limits?

The classification process itself should not include such indirect costs as management, clerical, and other support because they do not relate to direct care. Therefore, a separate indirect standard should be developed and monitored. This is not to suggest that the system disparages it but that it is identified as a unique and separate component with its own characteristics and factors that must be monitored in the management and support context rather than that of clinical practice.

This approach in the financial planning process helps the nurse manager to define and refine the costs of services and for monitoring and controlling these variables. This prevents the confusion that can arise in allocating costs between indirect and direct categories.

A careful, systematic, meaningful, and accurate approach to the development of a patient acuity and classification system can provide the manager with a sound data base for herself and her clinical colleagues. This will go far to support the appropriate utilization of financial resources and long-range financial planning for the unit, department, or nursing service.

SUGGESTED READING

Anderson, R.N., and James Reese. *Accounting Principles,* 5th Ed. Homewood, Ill.: Richard D. Irwin, Inc., 1983.

Curtain, Leah, and Carolina Zurlage. *DRGs: The Reorganization Of Health.* Chicago: S-N Publications, 1984.

Hepner, James. *Health Planning for Emerging Multihospital Systems.* St. Louis: The C.V. Mosby Company, 1978.

Klein, David. "Plan Accounting Systems for Special Needs," *Management Focus* (March–April, 1979): 22–25.

National League for Nursing, *Perspectives in Nursing, 1983–1985; 1985–1987.* New York: Author, 1983, 1985.

Supply and Operating Costs

OBJECTIVES FOR CHAPTER 6

This chapter will:
1. *Outline cost accounting characteristics and their application to the management of supply and operational costs.*
2. *Profile specific patient costs and account and resource budgetary approaches.*
3. *Identify the process of cost estimation and its use in budget planning.*
4. *Review the use of financial statistical processes in budget planning.*
5. *Identify simple graphing techniques for the presentation of historical data.*
6. *Discuss the use of graphic and statistical processes for forecasting and projecting for budgetary planning.*
7. *Identify sample line items and the process of preparation in the nursing budgeting framework.*

It is of course true that human resources are at the heart of any service or department. Control of operating costs, however, supplies the meat and potatoes of any institution. Without the necessary support, no function can be carried out adequately regardless of the personnel talent available.

The operational items in the budget and financing of the service or department must receive the detailed analysis that they deserve and that can make the difference in an efficient and well-designed financial plan. With the rise in governmental and public sensitivity to costs related to patient care, nurse managers must have a solid understanding of the operational costs framework.

COST ACCOUNTING

A relatively new approach has emerged for building a financial plan at the nursing departmental or service level that is different from the traditional method. Over the years, most of the account items were those identified in a general ledger of accounts in the business office. While the mechanism for accounts listing of operational items has not changed, the financial planning for such items is being designed in a new way. The departmental or service financial planner and the nurse manager should start by identifying costs associated directly with patients or cases receiving services.

The goal is to put together a picture of each individual case and to build an information base involving similar cases so as to ascertain their cost norms. As noted earlier, building this data base helps the manager to know the normal expenditures of her service and for patients.

Much of the data needed to undertake a patient or case accounts approach to clinical management may not yet be available to the manager in the appropriate format. Most nursing organizations do not correlate data by patient care account. Those that use nursing cost accounting have not done so long enough for a definitive pattern to emerge. The goal, however, is to begin. If the manager did not begin yesterday, the time to begin is today.

The design phase is always the best place to start. This involves tying together the various components of the nursing financial plan based on such items as nursing care mix, such as by diagnosis related group (DRG). The billing system itemizes costs in each patient's account. In the past, the major problem was the limited ability to gather patient-specific data for particular illnesses. That changed drastically with the advent of DRGs and prospective payment systems. Such information is necessary to determine total per-unit costs.

The nurse manager at the outset will have substantial data but often not in the correct format. As she goes through items one at a time, a picture of the process will emerge. Most of the data will be generated in such a way that they can be reported as line items on a per-patient or per-case basis. Like items then can be compared and combined in an account in order to evaluate their performance (see Exhibit 6-1).

Structuring the budget process is a key to accomplishing financial planning goals. The nurse manager must be able to identify expenses individually as well as by category of service. Expense categories should be defined narrowly. The manager often has found difficulty controlling supply items because they are classified with other like supply items (such as medical-surgical supplies) and thus are not accounted for individually.

When variances develop, the manager may find that the categories of supply expense are so broad that she cannot find the specific issue at the root of the problem. The chart of accounts, which identifies by number all items for which there

Exhibit 6-1 Patient Cost Profile

Patient Account: 013579	
DRG: 90	
Diagnosis: Pneumonia	

Items	Costs
Room	$900
Nursing Care	$560
Laboratory	$286
Radiology	$476
Respiratory	$201
Supplies	$310
Pharmacy	$104
Total	$2,837
Price Cap	$2,700
Deficit	$ 137

is a charge, should be so designed that it assists, not hinders, the manager. She should expect the supply or resource items to be identified in such a manner that she can locate them easily when needed to plan and control the budget process.

In supply management, a per-item charge will indicate value. The item value can be matched to the case (or service statistic), and multiplied by all similar items to give its total cost to the service or department. Items also can be matched with cases so that when totaled they will constitute the resources used, by case. This kind of double-ended statistic will help the manager plan both total and individual budget figures. (See Exhibit 6-2 for a summary account of resource use.)

ZERO-BASED BUDGETING, BUDGETING BY EXCEPTION, AND HISTORIC APPROACHES

There are a wide variety of approaches to the supply and support budgeting process. In an era of potentially changing variables, the nurse manager's best approach is to base as much as possible of the supply budget plan on service projections. Since almost all of the components of the financial plan involve a patient or case approach, it is appropriate to consider the supply budget in the same way.

Zero-based budgeting and budgeting by exception have been popular in recent decades. These approaches force services to analyze performance and to determine if they are adequate, necessary, or should even be continued. Each service or program must be analyzed and, when necessary, renegotiated every budget period and justified on its own current operating merits and value to the goals of the institution. Options for alternative cost-effective ways of providing services

Exhibit 6-2 Account Resource Use Summary

Patient Account: 1468001		
DRG: 90		
Nursing Diagnosis: 46		
35		
28		
67		
Account Item List		
IV Therapy		$1,055.23
Pharmacy Medication		2,063.46
Dressings		693.12
Floor Stock		1,389.25
Sugar Testing Kit		465.78
Personal Hygiene		132.45
Radiology		1,003.78
Laboratory		1,894.43
Dietary		456.78
Central Supply		567.21
	Total	$9,721.49

are assessed to determine whether they are appropriate in structure and function to be maintained and funded.

As popular as both these approaches have been, much of what is involved in a department or service budget is endemic to the service itself. The financial framework for nursing changes frequently, regardless of the degree of analysis or the alternatives. Since a budget should be built from the ground up, zero-based concepts always can be applied. However, historical and clinical data are too important in her nursing clinical framework to be put to only limited use. Indeed, in nursing, the historic and clinical factors often have the greatest impact on the financial planning process.

This is not to say that zero-based budgeting or budgeting by exception do not utilize data sources; they do, and necessarily so. However, it is desirable to apply a mix of concepts to the clinical budget planning process based on successful or validated clinical approaches. Building the budget can use zero-based principles; monitoring and maintaining the budget can use budgeting by exception principles.

The number of cases or other service factors should be a guiding statistic in determining the number of supply items. Again, the need for an integrated data base is important. The nurse manager should have determined through her historic data a relationship between acuity and resource use. The important consideration here is that she understand what that relationship is and be able to account for the items used in a case and, by extension, all similar cases. In this way, she uses her intensity index, case data, and resource data to identify the pattern of supply use per case. Her historical data cover the emergence of the relationship and can help her make decisions about that relationship in her planning.

Each setting has its own process for supply item identification and budgeting. If the only system available to a manager simply lists supply items alphabetically and gives their individual unit costs, that methodology can be used in the budget planning process. If, on the other hand, the nurse manager can look at supply items as a part of the data presentation in the context of cases, she has a better idea of the budgeting framework in which she can operate.

For example, if budgeting by DRG categories, she can identify each of the individual items within the category and establish each one's relationship with its cost. The total costs of the item within a DRG category then can be summed. Those cost parameters, plus an inflation factor as required, can be used to determine the expenses of a service or department in budget planning for a specific DRG category.

If the nurse manager has additional data on the cases her unit serves, their DRG categories, and her staffing and human resource statistics, she can obtain the total operational requirements of each DRG and budget accordingly.

Not every kind of supply item fits neatly into the case or service statistic category. Supply items cover a range of material from IV poles to wheelchairs, to monitors, unit computers, etc. Each of these is used in direct patient care delivery. However, the mechanism for incorporating the cost of their use into each DRG category is complex, so other methods must be used to determine the cost and value of supplies not expended directly for specific patient cases for which there will be a charge. Where possible, a service-related charge can be applied for the use of specific equipment such as monitors, special pumps, etc. Their cost then can be related directly to service use.

Some items such as wheelchairs may be more difficult to tie to resource use. They may have to be related to each case's costs and, if included as a capital purchase, a certain amount of the payment for services will be allocated to that capital item. There thus will be an indirect relationship between the service statistic and the individual supply item.

Supply items must be identified in terms of their cost and their relation to the patient care process, to the support of the system, or to the indirect care needs of the nursing service. The most reasonable predictor of that cost should be specified for each account. Again, historical data should help the nurse manager establish the relation between the supply item, case, or procedure, and the general direct or indirect costs related to the procedure.

ESTIMATING COSTS

Estimating costs is a predictive process that is relatively difficult. This function is an important part of the manager's financial role. She must have the ability to estimate costs effectively so that sound decisions can be made.

Two basic kinds of costs drive operations: fixed and variable. Each has its own set of complexities that makes it unique in cost estimating. Fixed costs are those that must be paid, regardless of any change in units of service or services delivered. They include taxes, rent (or mortgage), interest, etc. They generally have little or no relationship to volume. Variable costs, on the other hand, respond to changes in volume. Variable costs include, for example, supplies that are related to the volume of utilization (such as IV fluids, dressing sets, and the like). In health care organizations, such costs can be both highly variable (with steep inclines or declines) or less volatile and thus slow to change (see Figure 6-1).

Of course, in actuality, nothing is completely black or white, so there also are partially variable costs. They may have a component that is fixed but may increase under certain circumstances. The gas or electric bill is an example: It has both a fixed component (rate) and a variable component (actual use).

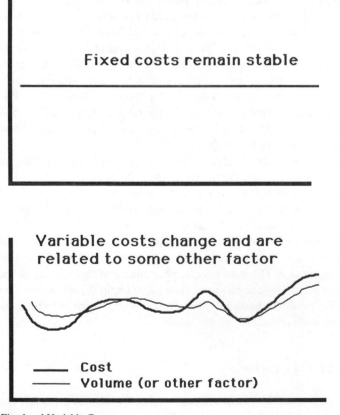

Figure 6-1 Fixed and Variable Costs

Another type of variable is the step function or semifixed cost that has a unique pattern of its own. That pattern shows a step-like increase as volume changes. In nursing, this could involve staffing that may require specific changes in volume that lead to a step-like change in staffing (see Figure 6-2).

The nurse manager must be aware of the cost constraints under which she operates. She must be able to identify which costs are fixed and which are variable. Variable costs in nurse staffing and service will demand a nursing systems response.

COSTS AND INFLATION

Inflation is a particular concern to the manager in estimating costs in her financial plan because it has a real impact on determining the true value of her

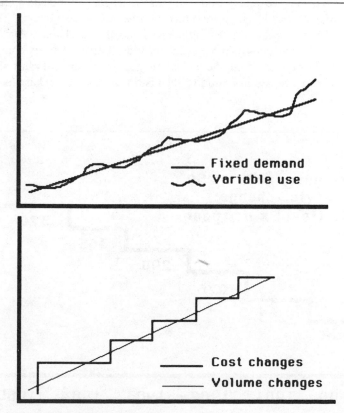

Figure 6-2 Examples of Step Function Changes

expenses. It is here that fixed and variable costs lose their clear distinction. Because of inflation, even fixed costs are not truly fixed.

There are many ways of understanding inflation. One is the use of such national measures as the consumer price index and its market basket of specified goods, with costs predicated on a base year against which all subsequent years are evaluated. Other measures involve medical and business prices.

The financial department usually monitors these indicators as they affect the health care instutitions and decides on a specific percent of inflation that it will use for a given budget period. That department also can provide rates or measure changes for specific costs in a particular nursing service.

For instance, the cost of the same number of cases in 1986 would be different from 1980 even if the patient population or the service characteristics did not change. If the cost in 1980 was $150,000; the institution arbitrarily established an inflation index at 250; if in 1986 the index registered 319, the significant change in the cost base would be obvious. By keeping track of annual changes in the index over the five-year period, the nurse manager can include a reasonably accurate inflation (or change in cost) factor for her subsequent budget. The nurse manager should note that the real inflation often varies each year. Although the example used here is a constant 5 percent per year, the rate can vary considerably and must be incorporated into the annual budget calculations. It must also comprise the appropriate rates for building the historical information base (see Figure 6-3).

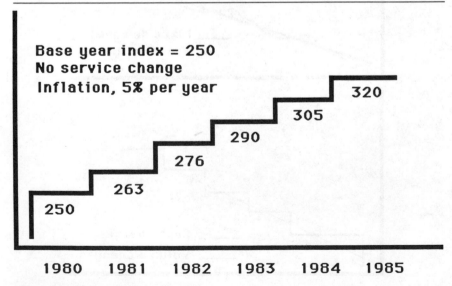

Base year index = 250
No service change
Inflation, 5% per year

320

305

290

276

263

250

1980   1981   1982   1983   1984   1985

Figure 6-3 Increases in Inflation Rates

ANALYSIS TECHNIQUES

The nursing manager cannot carry out her operational responsibility without including statistical and analytical abilities in her role as financial planner. Data analysis helps her assess the current situation and the environment and circumstances in which she will plan her budget.

Some analytical techniques are more useful than others. The nurse manager should not become an analyst or a statistical specialist. However, she must use available tools to undertake such analytical activities as are appropriate. This can help her in the budget construction process.

Simple linear regression can help the manager look at historical data and estimate which factors involve fixed costs or variable costs. Assessment of individual items provides too narrow a picture to enable her to determine the proportion of fixed and variable costs so they can be allocated to appropriate patient charges.

Simple linear regression merely means the presentation of data in a way that shows the relationship between two variables. A cost statistic and a service statistic are the variables used most commonly in a linear presentation in health care. The two axes on a diagram—horizontal and vertical—provide an opportunity to graph the relationship of the items being measured.

If the total cost of an item is related to the amount of service provided, then there should be a direct and simple acceleration or incline of both the costs and the number of items used. In simple linear regression, only one independent variable creates a relationship. Obviously, the more volume of use for a particular item, the more it costs in total; the more units of service delivered, the higher the total cost for its use; and the more patients served, the higher the total cost for providing that service (see Figure 6-4).

Items of analysis often are not easily or simply combined yet the nurse manager must do so to be able to make meaningful decisions on costs in relation to items. For example, the nurse manager of an outpatient service expects client visits in the next year to rise from 10,000 to 12,000. The question is whether the costs involved will increase by the same percentage as the number of patient visits— that is, by 20 percent.

However, it should be noted that the only ones that will increase 20 percent will be variable costs; fixed costs should not rise 20 percent since they do not move as a result of volume changes. Variable costs related to an increase in volume will move by a percent proportional to that volume change.

The nurse manager must realize that some of the variable expenses will not increase at a stable rate in any given year for a number of reasons. Nursing activities related to the delivery of care may change, depending on the patient, kind of service, and time it was delivered. These variables can be presented together in a scatter diagram or chart that looks at total costs over volume and associated factors. This shows the cost increase in relation to the volume increase. Since a

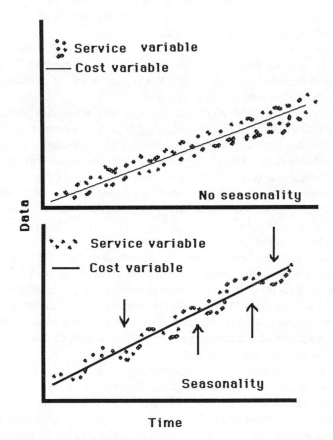

Figure 6-4 Linear Regression Trend Forecasts

regression analysis is being used as a predictor, the relation between total costs, volume, and other factors in the care process is shown by locating them near the straight line through the midpoint of the scattergram. This gives an idea of the best estimate of cost related to other influencing considerations (see Figure 6-5).

An explanation of the use of linear and other regression techniques can always be found in statistical or accounting management texts (see Suggested Reading at

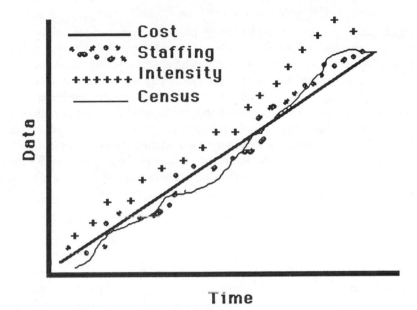

Figure 6-5 Multiple Variables Influencing Cost

---

end of chapter); these can help the nurse manager with the techniques of using such analysis in budget decisions. This book does not delve deeply into these statistical processes; rather, it identifies for the nurse manager the simple and complex statistical processes available to help her validate judgments and data in order to make more meaningful decisions.

A more complex measure is called multiple regression analysis. This is a sophisticated process that can call together a number of independent or highly variable data sources. These can be independent or variable, often both, operating together to influence any of a number of budget planning factors. Such formulas account for fixed costs, multiple variable costs, proportional variable costs, all costs attributable to single items or situations, and costs attributable to higher cost variabilities when related to volume. Multiple regression analysis should be used with a financial computer or data center.

Reliance on statistical approaches is up to the nurse manager. Statistical models are designed to help her make decisions on the outlay of operational dollars for goods and services for her specific clinical entity. The use of variable analytical methods will help her look at large amounts of data, ascertain their relationship, and build a budget on as accurate as possible a projection of those relationships.

A major part of the operational budgeting process depends on the ability successfully to anticipate and predict costs based on statistical and analytical tools. A number of approaches are available, many of them related to regression analysis and other statistical techniques. It is the responsibility of the nurse manager to decide which techniques are appropriate for her service and her particular analytical needs. The nurse manager can use appropriate analytical and/or statistical texts or data and computer systems to assemble complex information related to her fixed and variable expenses, determine their relation, and define the impact of one upon the other. Using these estimates, she can establish a baseline for the forecasting mechanisms to determine the kind of data needed and their relation to her service and budget projections.

FORECASTING

Much of what forecasting involves has been discussed in previous chapters. Beyond that, the technique of presenting data, then making decisions based on what the presentation shows, is an important part of the nurse manager's forecasting in the budget planning process. Here again, translating information into data that represent activity and historical processes, then analyzing them, can assist the nurse manager's decisionmaking.

The Use of Graphs

Graphic presentation of data is perhaps the most effective way the nurse manager can help make decisions. Data in graphs or tables allow her to look at a whole complex of data bases in simplified form and to make decisions about what they reveal. In most graphed presentations of nursing data, the vertical axis represents the measurable item (usually the variable) and the horizontal axis the time period (usually the fixed item). The volume or work-related item eventually will become a predictor of changes and thus is the statistic of greatest importance.

Almost all data can be presented in graph form. The graph gives the nurse manager a visual presentation of the relationship of the various elements over a time continuum. She wants to determine whether there is any particular trend, relationship, seasonal, or monthly variables in the data that indicates whether she must respond. The fluctuations in the data denote meaningful points in the distribution and utilization of services or materials and supplies.

The pattern of a graph should give an indication of consistency, continuity, or general tendency that shows the nurse manager the flow of information over the defined time. Breaking the time spans into quarters, months, or even shorter periods relates each of those individualized periods to the overall time. For example, quarterly trends and projections can be compared with the annualized data. The longer the time frame the graph represents, the better its accuracy over the period; the shorter the time, the lower the confidence in long-term projections.

The variabilities shown should have an impact on the nurse manager's planning. If there is a characteristic trend that flows clearly over the time represented, she can make relatively simple judgments; however, if the fluctuations are severe, the pattern of components as displayed becomes more important.

Identifying whether fluctuation is random, indicates a generalized trend, or is variable or seasonal are important considerations. Random fluctuations show no significant relation of items with each other or with the time frame in which they have been graphed. Trend items should show a significant and continuous relationship between the items over time. The manager can locate key points on the graph and compare them with other points, using that comparison to indicate a trend relationship. Monthly, seasonal, or annual trends that appear on the graph can guide the manager's decisions.

Trend Recognition

One of the most important aspects of the manager's data interpretation is her recognition of where trends exist. Once she has discerned a trend, its cause or its relation to the nursing service becomes an important basis for her judgment as to its impact.

For example, if utilization of supplies has increased at a 4 percent rate over a two-year period but the service projection has risen at an 8 percent rate and the rate appears continuous in the graph, the nurse manager can decide that there is some relationship between the costs and services depicted. She probably will have to lower her projection if the actual cost increase remains at half the percent increase estimated.

The nurse manager's decisions derived from the graphs then become a part of the data base that she uses in planning. She can have a high level of confidence in basing future decisions on these data—barring factors such as inflation, uncontrolled market forces, item cost increases, or other data adjustments.

Regional, quarterly, semiannual, or seasonal data usually become more valuable when reviewed in graph form. Patterns begin to appear that can be the basis for defining relationships between the nursing service and the statistics. The allocation of materials, human resources, and supplies may be highly dependent upon the use of those supplies during the time period in which the trends occur. If seasonal trends indicate that utilization is lower during the summer months, then the distribution of budgeted and planned services must reflect that fact—all other things remaining equal.

The nurse manager must analyze the graphs carefully because trends might not always be visible immediately. Depending upon the amount of data, she may have to determine not only the relation between components but its degree and its changes over the period represented by the graph.

Sometimes the graph produces a combination effect for which the nurse manager must be alert. Time and trend changes may occur in conjunction with each other. For instance, there may be seasonal changes in service projections as well as in trends. The seasonal change in spring (for example, an increase) may be different from the one in the fall (for example, a decrease), but all seasonal changes over a defined time may indicate an overall growth in service. In such a case, both the season and the trend operate in conjunction with each other.

Graphs in Budget Planning

Graphs are helpful in budget planning. However, it is equally important to apply basic arithmetic in interpreting graphs to determine the accuracy and degree of the relationships of the variables. Seasonal or time variables, as noted, do not always occur in fixed patterns. Some variance might occur in March of one year and in February (or April) of the next year.

Determining an average figure, in this example, by adding the three-month totals for the past three- to five-year historical period, then dividing them by nine (for three years) or by 15 (for five years) will give a fairly accurate prediction for one of the months. Moving average predictions give a more accurate indicator of the appropriate decision than do static projections.

Trends can be viewed in the same context. Sometimes the meaning or even the possibility of a trend may not be clear on visual review. Again, regression techniques help interpret where a trend might appear. Through the use of computers or calculators, a relationship can be established between X and Y variables, X being the item and Y being the amount. Establishment of that relationship begins to create a second graph that shows a more direct relation between the time period and the variable items, in this case time being indicated by the Y axis and the variable of volume or item number by the X axis. Marking the individual items on the graph at the time they appear can give the nurse manager some idea of the trend relationship that might not have been as clear when presented simply as a volume item over a defined time factor.

Statistical Approaches

A number of statistical approaches can be utilized to validate the visual and graphic factors. Overlaying data upon others can help establish the relationship of one data base to another, such as nursing staffing levels with patient census levels if the goal is to determine such a match. This technique also helps establish relationships between graphic presentation and the trends that they might indicate when compared.

The standard deviation can be used to determine appropriate response ranges to data, especially in relation to staffing and volume. With this technique, the range of data presentation may indicate the parameters within which a manager may want to act in terms of budget planning for staffing or other like resource expenses.

In standard deviation, the time to be covered by the graph must be determined and related to the item measured. In this case that may be a census variable. Such a calculation includes the mean for that variable minus its mean and a census variable minus its mean, squared. When this total has been determined and divided by its square root, the square root product is the standard deviation range for the mean or displayed data. This range then can be used to determine the relationship, in this example, between census needs and staffing levels (see Figure 6-6).

Forecasting provides wide latitude for the nurse manager in making budget planning decisions. This involves using historical data as a basis for a more accurate presentation of her financial plan.

OPERATIONAL EXPENSE ITEMS

As indicated earlier, all operational items involving supplies, materials, and other service-related goods should be related to the individual service category. Some costs that do not seem to be clearly linked to individual service categories—outside personnel, education, dues, subscriptions, meetings, travel, etc.—still are important to nursing and must be calculated in the operating budget. The mechanisms for doing so may vary broadly, depending on the institution and its particular way of expensing these categories. However, each of these items is significant for the nursing service (see Exercise 6-1 in Appendix 6-A).

As noted, the use of outside personnel is based on scheduled variances and other anomalies. Institutions should strive to keep this use low since outside personnel are expensive and their quality can vary. Budgeting for outside personnel is based on the historic pattern of need and its projection to the future.

Factors the nurse manager must consider include the category of worker being budgeted, the agency or contract under which such services are provided, the rate per hour or per period, the number of hours being utilized, the total of the rate times the hours, and the total monthly amount being spent for outside personnel. This expense may be (1) allocated specifically to the DRG category if the institution's accounting mechanism permits it or (2) related generally to the service, then divided proportionately into each of the categories.

Formula:

$$g = \sqrt{\frac{n(\Sigma x^2) - (\Sigma x)^2}{n^2}}$$

Number of beds: 30

Range of occupancy: 18–25

Number of days occupied: 365

n = 365 (days) Σx = 7920 (total patients)

Σx^2 = 173000

Calculation:

$$365\frac{(173000) - (7920)^2}{365^2} = \frac{63145000 - 62726400}{133225}$$

$$\sqrt{3.14} = s\ 1.77$$

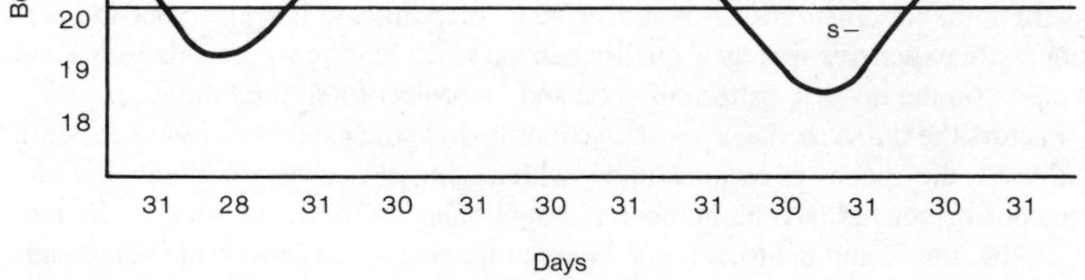

Figure 6-6 Using Standard Deviation for Developing a Staffing Range

The first mechanism obviously is the most accurate and most appropriate because those utilizing the services of outside personnel would be charged directly. However, some managers argue that since these services are a part of the institution's menu of offerings, they should not be allocated directly to the patient (see Exercise 6-2 in Appendix 6-A).

MEETINGS AND TRAVEL

All professionals must be involved in professional continuing education. Maintaining competence is an important part of professional responsibility. Much of the time this is not available within the institution, although the facility assumes some obligation. The nurse manager thus must budget for meetings and travel time outside the institution. Such expenditures must be justified in detail since every institution puts a limit on them.

Managers must be fair in how they allocate funds for meetings and travel to make sure they are distributed equitably among the eligible practitioners. This also should be based on the needs of the service, the requirements of individuals in meeting those needs, and their specific competency and learning needs. There usually are other rules regarding distance from the institution, amount of money spent for food, lodging, transportation, etc., that must be incorporated into the budgeting process.

The nurse manager must consider all of these factors. Her meeting and travel expense budget will show specifically the month in which the expense is to be incurred, the individual(s) involved, the reason for travel, the destination, registration fee, food, lodging, transportation, and other considerations. These of course are added to give the total expense for each instance. Monthly and annual totals then are derived. The nurse manager reviews these data to determine whether the expenditures were within budget and were distributed appropriately among the staff members (see Exercises 6-3 and 6-7 in Appendix 6-A).

INTERNAL MEETINGS

The business of nursing also involves expenses for in-house committees and educational meetings. Again, most institutions offer in-house educational opportunities to their staff members to help them maintain competence.

Institutions must maintain detailed records on educational and committee work because they take up valuable time and should be meaningful. It also is expensive time since the dollars paid often are not related directly to patient care. Historical data can help guide the allocation of dollars and personnel for specific committee and education time. Since most health care institutions operate primarily in decentralized approaches to cost accounting, meeting and education time should be as specific a cost as possible. The ability to articulate clearly the individual cost for each educational session as well as for each committee meeting and the total value of those processes is an important part of the planning strategy of the manager. Since it is her goal to have a complete understanding of all of the expenses in her service, knowing the amount of money allocated for committees and educational time on an internal basis will be an important part of her control function. Such activities should relate specifically to advancing the goals and objectives of the institution or service. In turn, they should be provided for when determining those objectives.

Expense records for committee and educational meetings should include the monthly allocation of time, the name of the event, and anticipated attendance, food, meals, supplies, accommodations, etc. If outside speakers are planned, their fees must be included. The statistics on meeting time can be compared with clinical and other productive time to show the proportionate utilization (see Exercise 6-4 in Appendix 6-A).

MINOR EQUIPMENT

Some expenses in the nursing service or unit are less than capital expenditures but do fall within specified categories of costs for minor equipment. Minor equipment includes items costing less than the institution's level for a capital expense. For instance, if $5,000 is the bottom limit of the capital expenditure category, any item below that would come under the minor equipment expense category.

All equipment has a life span, so the nurse manager should be prepared when new pieces are needed. Because equipment planning is an important part of her function, she should be well acquainted with the kinds of equipment on the market. Most equipment should be designed to make the work of nursing easier, more productive, and more effective, and provide better patient care or comfort.

The nurse manager must budget for minor equipment just as carefully as for major equipment. The purchase of minor equipment must be justified and its value to the service understood.

Because a large number of minor equipment items can comprise a major component of the budget, such equipment should be prioritized, with items essential for the nursing service acquired first. All items should have a time payment schedule to spread the cost across the budget period. Again, records must show the date of purchase, name and kind of equipment, vendor, reason for purchase, maintenance agreements and other such considerations, total cost, monthly cost, and total expenditure for the budget period.

As with capital equipment, minor equipment expenses usually are in competition with requests by other services, divisions, departments, or units. Therefore, the better the justification for minor equipment, the better the chances are of obtaining it. The competitive nature of the financial plan should be a consideration of the nurse manager. If another unit or service is requesting a similar piece of equipment that can be shared, it is good strategy for both managers together to justify and defend its acquisition. This avoids duplication (see Exercise 6-5 in Appendix 6-A).

The same process should be followed when equipment is to be rented. The justification for the equipment rental should include the kind of item, the reason for rental rather than purchase, the month in which it is to be rented, and the rental charges (see Exercise 6-6 in Appendix 6-A).

DUES AND SUBSCRIPTIONS

Most institutions employing primarily professional workers have a mechanism for supporting their activities in professional organizations (dues, travel, etc.) or through subscriptions to specialty journals. Institutions are committed to offering the highest level of nursing services, in part by supporting practitioners in acquiring or enhancing skills and information they may need. Funds for this are allocated in the operational budget.

Again, institutions, services and units must have specified limits as to the total available for dues. The nursing manager and the nursing staff must understand these dollar limits. When such expenditures are approved, the record should identify the individual and the professional organization, and the month dues are paid.

This same basic process holds true for subscriptions. When they are approved, the record should show the month in which they are allocated for payment, the publisher, the name of the journal, staff utilization of the publication, the total amount allocated for it, and the total monthly allocations for all journals for the nursing unit.

As institutions tighten their controls on everything that does not relate specifically to delivery of patient services, they tend to put responsibility on each professional to subscribe to her own journals and participate in organizations without institutional support. Indeed, in an era of increasing cost containment, such areas are early targets when budgets are cut. However, if the institution is committed to participating in such efforts, careful allocation and responsible use of dollars by the individual units or services can help assure that the support will be maintained. When such expenditures go over budget, they create a negative attitude in the institution and the unit risks losing the support. Since such benefits can be justified, it is the responsibility of the nurse manager to assure that they are controlled appropriately (see Exercises 6-8 and 6-9 in Appendix 6-A).

PURCHASED SERVICES

At times, an individual service or unit may require short-term specialized professional or corporate direct or consulting services. Such purchased services may be on a one-time basis and need be allocated only once in the budgeting process. They can be related to program developments, alterations, and services, or consultations for specific programs, plans, or undertakings.

Purchased services may be continuing ones provided to a unit by other professionals such as psychologists, specially trained nurses, and others. These individuals may not be employees of the institution, so purchased services become the mechanism of choice. When such additional services are approved, the record should include the kinds of services, the month in which they are provided, the time required, who provides them, the reason, and the monthly and overall total.

Since many nursing organizations are using an ever-wider array of professionals, the use of a purchased (or external) service category in the budget is gaining in importance. The nurse manager must determine the costs and justify the need for the service. She also must decide whether purchased services under contractual arrangements or employee services would be more cost effective or more desirable, given her budget constraints (see Exercises 6-10 and 6-11 in Appendix 6-A).

SUMMARY

The allocation of operational expenses obviously is an integral part of the budget planning process. The nurse manager's responsibility is not only to understand the way in which these expenses can be estimated and accounted for, but also to determine how best to determine how many dollars should be directed to which operational components, based on historical and current data.

The nurse manager must understand the cost-accounting process in allocating operational expenses and in budget planning. Items that are not strictly services must be accounted for. Expenses such as educational, meeting, travel, dues, subscriptions, purchased services, minor equipment, etc., must be identified and costed as appropriate to the department, service, or unit. The manager must be able to justify their cost.

The budgeting process should reflect efforts to meet the institution's goals and objectives. Since the operational expenses support the services provided, they should have a direct correlation with the needs of those services. The nurse manager's effectiveness will be measured by how well she can integrate her department's operational expenses with the goals and objectives yet stay within the budget.

SUGGESTED READING

Ameiss, Albert, and Nicholas Kargas. *Accountants Desk Handbook.* Englewood Cliffs, N.J.: Prentice-Hall, Inc., 1980.

Finkler, Stephen. *Budgeting Concepts for Nurse Managers.* Orlando, Fla.: Grune & Stratton, Inc., 1984, 87–175.

Harmer, Gary. "Bridging the GAAP Between Budgeting and Accounting." *Governmental Finance* (March 1981): 19–24.

Horngren, Charles. *Accounting for Management Control: An Introduction.* Englewood Cliffs, N.J.: Prentice-Hall, Inc., 1965.

Smith, H. W. *Strategies of Social Research.* Englewood Cliffs, N.J.: Prentice-Hall, Inc., 1975, 315–340.

Appendix 6-A

Exercise and Practice Tools

Exercise 6-1 General Budget

G-11 OPERATING EXPENSE BUDGET
Zero-Based—*General*

Responsibility Center:

Name: _____

Number: _____

Natural Expense Account Number: _____
Natural Expense Account Name: _____

Month	Item or Event	Amount	Month Total
		Total	

Exercise 6-2 Outside Personnel

Responsibility Center:

Name: _____

Number: _____

G-1 OPERATING EXPENSE BUDGET
Zero-Based—*Outside Personnel 092*

Month	Category of Worker	Agency/Source	A Rate/Hr.	B Hours	Total A × B	Monthly Amount
					Total	

Exercise 6-3 Meetings and Travel

Responsibility Center:

Name: _____

Number: _____

G-2 OPERATING EXPENSE BUDGET
Zero-Based—*Meetings and Travel 300*

Month	Traveler	Destination & Reason	A Regis.	B Food & Lodging	C Transportation	(A + B + C) Total	Monthly Total

Total

Exercise 6-4 Internal Meetings

Responsibility Center:

Name: _____

Number: _____

G-3 OPERATING EXPENSE BUDGET
Zero-Based—*Internal Meetings 302*

Month	Meeting	A No. Attending	B Food Rate*	(A + B = C) Food Total	D Supplies Total	E Accom. Total	(C + D + E) Meet. Total	Monthly Total
							Total	

*Food from Food Services (per person):   Total
Coffee $0.50   Hot Lunches $4.52
Coffee & Donuts $0.85   Dinner $10.20
Cold Lunch $3.85   Stand-Up Events $7.25

Exercise 6-5 Minor Equipment

Responsibility Center:

Name: _____

Number: _____

G-4 OPERATING EXPENSE BUDGET
Zero-Based—*Minor Equipment 355*

Month	Equipment	Vendor	Maintenance Agree. No. or Amt.*	Cost	Monthly Total
			Total	Total	

*If maintenance is not provided in the first-year warranty, enter the maintenance agreement cost anticipated for FY 198___ –8___.

Exercise 6-6 Equipment Rental

Responsibility Center:

Name: _____ _____

Number: _____ _____

G-10 OPERATING EXPENSE BUDGET
Zero-Based—*Equipment Rental 780*

Month	Equipment Item	Rent From	Reason	Amount	Month Total
				Total	

Exercise 6-7 Educational

G-5 OPERATING EXPENSE BUDGET
Zero-Based—*Educational 460*

Responsibility Center: _____

Name: _____

Number: _____

Month	Event	A No. Attending	B Food Rate*	(A + B = C) Food Total	D Books & Supp.	E Accom. Total	(C + D + E) Meet. Total	Monthly Total
							Total	

*Food from Food Services (per person): Total

Coffee $0.50	Hot Lunches $4.52	
Coffee & Donuts $0.85	Dinner $10.20	
Cold Lunches $3.85	Stand-Up Events $7.25	

Exercise 6-8 Dues

Responsibility Center:

Name: _____

Number: _____

G-6 OPERATING EXPENSE BUDGET
Zero-Based—*Dues 689*

Month	Member	Organization	Amount	Monthly Total

Total

Exercise 6-9 Subscriptions

Responsibility Center:

Name: _____ _____

Number: _____

G-7 OPERATING EXPENSE BUDGET
Zero-Based—Subscriptions 690

Month	Publication	Where Filed	Amount	Month Total

Total

Exercise 6-10 Purchased Services—Corporation

Responsibility Center:

Name: _____

Number: _____

G-8 OPERATING EXPENSE BUDGET

Zero-Based—*Purchased Services—Corporation 750*

Month	Service Purchased	From	Amount	Monthly Total
			Total	

Exercise 6-11 Purchased Services—Individual

Responsibility Center:

Name: _____

Number: _____

G-9 OPERATING EXPENSE BUDGET
Zero-Based—Purchased Services—Individual 751

Month	Service Purchased	From	Amount	Monthly Total

Total

Capital Budgeting and Planning

OBJECTIVES FOR CHAPTER 7

This chapter will:
1. *Review the basic elements of a capital budgeting process.*
2. *Outline the nurse manager's role in capital budgeting.*
3. *Identify the appropriate capital budgeting process.*
4. *Identify various characteristics of capital and its importance to the monetary value of the institution.*
5. *Discuss the preparation of various practice mechanisms to allow the nurse manager to develop her skills in capital budget operation.*

Capital budget planning is a highly complex process that involves many components of financial planning. The capital budget is essentially a blueprint for long-term investment in the institution. It can include items costing as much as several million dollars to those costing as little as $250 to $500. The key difference between a capital item and a noncapital item is that the former has an acquired asset value of a certain amount and a lifetime usually of more than one year.

The value of capital items can affect the institution's revenues. These revenues usually are received as a direct result of the investment in the capital items that relates to the revenues they produce. Since capital items are a long-term investment, the returns on them may not appear in their initial years but the overall return usually is expected to justify the outlay. Therefore, a review of capital budget investments is an appraisal of their value to the institution over their entire life. Decisions on capital purchases thus relate to the lifetime of the asset and to the value of that purchase to the institution.

Capital expenditures usually involve large sums of money. Many institutions do not have enough money to make major capital purchases all at one time. The capital budgeting process requires that choices be made as to the allocation of the funds available. The priorities and hierarchy of choices relate specifically to the goals and objectives of the institution. Capital expenditures undertaken by any institution, service, or department must be justified through a description of its program value, purchase time, cost, criteria for capital expenses, and its value to the facility over its life. Clearly then, a relationship exists between the capital budget plan and the cash budgeting process. The cash availability often will indicate the amount of capital investment that can be undertaken at any given time.

CASH BUDGET

An institution must have sufficient cash to meet its operating needs. Such requirements as paying bills and meeting payroll obligations are provided for in the cash budget process. However, it is unwise to keep too much of an institution's assets in cash beyond payroll and expense needs; instead, it should be invested to earn interest or be applied to reduce debts.

The nurse manager should be fully aware that management of the institution's cash is as important as that of any other component. The ability to manage its cash elements successfully make it possible for the institution to plan capital purchases. Therefore, reimbursement for patient services from the government, insurance companies, and other third party payers (and the schedule of those payments) provide the basis for determining cash flow. Under the new reimbursement and payment systems legislated in the mid-1980s, such payments usually include interest and depreciation. This adds to income.

In the purchase of a piece of capital equipment, more of the payments go for interest in the early years; later, as the balance is paid down, the payments go increasingly to reduce the principal. The financial manager and the nurse manager must consider this total picture of the equipment's life expectancy when purchasing and operating the acquisition. Still, technological development quickly changes the value of capital equipment, so that purchase of equipment is often risky. Buying a piece of equipment with a life of 10 years but that is obsolete in 3 years is not wise and has a negative effect on the institution.

In budget planning, the cash budget often is considered as an item separable from others. For the most part, cash budgeting and management are the responsibility of the finance department. However, the nurse manager must be aware of the influence of the cash budget on decisions made by her and others in managing the capital purchase planning process.

Most cash budgets operate in the same way, with the finance office reporting of cash balances monthly. Cash projections are made known at the beginning of each month. These include anticipated cash receipts, identified by account receivable and by payer. Monthly receipts are added to the accrued cash balance.

Total cash receipts and cash on hand are subtracted from the actual monthly disbursements and the amount remaining is the cash balance.

When the cash balance indicates a surplus for any long period, that surplus can be invested to earn interest. The final cash balance for any given month becomes the initial cash balance for the succeeding month, and the same sequence is repeated.

The finance manager analyzes the cash situation every month to determine variables that may indicate changes in the institution's operation or in its cash flow. Movement up or down of cash availability indicates the impact of operational expenses and other items. It therefore should be clear to the nurse manager how vital the relationship is between cash viability and the capital budgeting process.

She must realize that the value of money is highly variable, depending on the economic circumstances. Managing money thus is a crucial part in the budgeting process. The more money the institution has to invest, the more opportunity it has to increase its value by collecting interest; the more it must expend for payment of purchases, the less it has to invest and the greater the chance of a loss.

Capital budgeting is much like basic investment planning. A capital purchase essentially is an investment opportunity for the organization. Therefore, the institution must consider just how much of an opportunity a capital purchase is and compare that with other investment alternatives.

For example, if the institution can invest $500 in a piece of capital equipment and receive $800 of value over a seven-year lifetime, the question becomes: Will the purchase of the equipment be a better yield on dollars invested than some alternative purchase or investment over the same period. Such choices are complex and demand careful consideration. If money can be invested at a rate of interest higher than what can be gained through the purchase of a capital item and the asset is not in itself sufficiently revenue producing to offset the cost of the investment, then perhaps investment in mutual funds, bank accounts, Federal notes or other kinds of financial instruments may yield more value to the institution over the same period.

It is the job of the finance department to weigh these factors to assure that the institution is advantaged by whatever decisions are made and that such gains are determined in light of the need for capital equipment. The institution must be able to maintain its service and its competitiveness and upgrade its equipment to meet quality and growth demands to compete in the marketplace. It must have state-of-the-art facilities to meet its needs, goals, and objectives.

The finance office also looks at departmental capital budgeting proposals and processes within a multidepartmental or institutional systems framework. The processes should be tied into the institution's needs. Capital purchases that may benefit an individual department may be of no significant value to the institution as a whole. It then becomes important that the finance department analyze each individual capital budget request in the context of the overall process and its relationship to the goals of the institution and approve the most appropriate ones. Factors it evaluates include (1) net present value, which determines whether a capital asset earns more or less than an anticipated rate of return; or (2) an internal rate of return that shows whether the equipment or other item is earning more or less than projected.

The time value of money also is an important consideration because it can have an impact on the desirability of certain capital budgeting projects and how much they can return to the institution. Time value of money means the value of money over any period of time and is determined by how it is managed. If money is invested, interest can be earned. If it is spent as cash for equipment purchase, for example, interest due on borrowed money for this purpose is avoided. How money is spent and received indicates how much will be gained or lost.

Another mechanism is the present cost approach, which considers the present value of the costs of a variety of approaches for capital projects and compares them in order to determine whether they accomplish the same goal. Obviously, a project that has the least negative impact on the total overall costs of the institution would be the most desirable choice. This approach is used when commitment to the capital project is clear. It provides the opportunity to choose the approach with the smallest lifetime cost.

All these methodologies and other statistical and mathematical approaches to capital budgeting are a major responsibility of the finance office. The nurse manager, for her part, must understand that there are many considerations involved in the capital budgeting processes. She must relate her own capital proposals to the much larger goals of the entire institution.

THE DEPARTMENT MANAGER'S ROLE

The nurse manager's role in capital budget planning involves developing proposals consonant with the master plan that the institution will approve to enhance its growth. The same planning techniques discussed in earlier chapters must be applied.

The nurse manager must know what capital needs are vital for meeting the goals of her department consistent with the direction of the institution. This means specifically that the board and administration must provide that direction so that the nurse manager may focus on capital items that not only aid her service but also complement the institution's overall objectives.

She thus must develop her planning process in a logical and consistent manner:

1. The nurse manager must be familiar with the operational plan for the institution of which she is a part.

2. The nurse manager must be guided by the institution's policy, goals, and directions in her thinking regarding her service parameters and the capital expenditures she needs to meet those objectives.
3. The nurse manager must review the equipment, materials, and supplies essential to carry out her service objectives. She must identify the functional value of capital expenses. Comparative analysis of a variety of capital expense items from differing sources will help her focus on the cost, functional, and utilization issues related to the purchase of capital equipment.
4. The nurse manager must review with the materials management division, or directly with vendors and providers, appropriate costs of capital equipment.

She must determine whether a desired capital item is appropriate to the needs of her service and consistent with the overall direction of the institution. She can use a problem-oriented approach to ascertaining the viability of particular capital purchases. In this approach, the nurse manager should describe the problem that is creating the need for the purchase and whether her department could provide the service without the capital item.

Hospital and medical staff members who might be affected by the capital expenditure should be involved in evaluating the needs and the difficulties created by the lack of the particular item of equipment as well as in defining the benefits, trade-offs, and alternatives within the context of the capital budget planning process. This input helps support the nurse manager's argument.

Presumably she already will have examined and discarded alternatives. She must assure that she is not proposing the item merely to avoid the extra effort that might be involved in using a less costly method.

This becomes important when she prepares to defend her request. When there is competition for a limited number of resources in the capital budget, the nurse manager must realize that her requests must convince administration that all alternatives have been considered, and why they were rejected.

The corollary is explaining why her proposal is the best possible solution. The nurse manager should relate the capital request to the operational processes that will attest the value of the equipment sought. She should attempt to make clear that any decision other than approval would be inappropriate.

Finally, the nurse manager should identify the costs of the item and of alternative solutions. It should be evident to the financial reviewer that the nurse manager has considered the alternatives and has a good handle on the total cost range of the item she requested. In this way, the reviewer can determine quickly that the nurse manager has considered all of the variables before choosing a specific item and it clearly is the best selection (see Exhibit 7-1 and Exercise 7-1 in Appendix 7-A).

Exhibit 7-1 Capital Budget

Responsibility Center: Clinical: ✓

Name: Nursing

Number: 987

C—CAPITAL BUDGET

FY 198__8__   Nonclinical:

Page 1 of 1

Expend. Class	Rev.? Y or N	Qty.	Vendor	Item or Project Description	Mo. of Order	Total Cost by Pay. or Proj. Comp. Date			Cost Source	Maint. Agree.
						4/8 – 9/8	10/8 – 3/8	Aft3/8		
C	Y	1	Picker	Oncology Center	4/8	$100,000	$1,250,000	$50,000	V	-0-
C	N	1	SJB	Renovation for Center	5/8		80,000		M	-0-
C	N	1	Steelcase	Model 1480 Desk w/type standard	1/8		800		P	-0-
B	N	4	Ericsson	Microfiche camera reader-printer unit (replaces Kodak Model 850)	2/8		5,000	15,000	E	$500
					Totals	100,000	1,335,800	65,000		

Submitted By: E.F.   Reviewed By: L.B.

The cost framework and the approach to determining the value of a capital item is an important process in assigning a priority to a request at both the institutional and departmental or unit levels. The institution should have a structure that prioritizes short-term and long-range capital item requests. These priorities should match the market and goal directives of the institution or department. This also will affect the timing of the purchase.

The administrative and financial officers will want to know specifically the projection of the most appropriate purchase times for capital items and how they can be spread over the budget period. Therefore, the nurse manager should incorporate such details in her proposal. The timing must relate to the goals of the service and of the institution.

For example, if an important new service need must be met in the short term, it is obvious that the capital item should be purchased as soon as possible. Items that can be delayed should be, consistent with the service requirements of the individual unit.

The planning process should require that the nurse manager develop a long-range capital budget for her department. This can alert the institution to some of the needs it must meet in the future. In the vastly changed health care environment of the late 1980s, managers have much shorter planning periods than a decade ago. It seems wise not to project service needs 3 to 5 years ahead.

Even so, there is no great confidence in the viability of 3- to 5-year projections. There is a whole new marketplace out there. However, the nurse manager should have an idea of where the service she is proposing will take her, and how long it will take. Rational projections discussed in earlier chapters should assist her in making decisions on the appropriateness of capital items related to new service projections (see Exhibit 7-2). Again, the items must be listed in priority so that the essential capital expenditures are clear to the manager and to the reviewer, especially those that can enhance the work of an individual service or unit (see Exercise 7-2).

Establishing priorities for capital items is difficult. The nurse manager finds that she needs most of the items listed in her capital expense budget if she is to provide certain kinds of service. The question often raised is not whether the capital item itself is essential but whether the use to which it is directed will become a component of the service mix already being offered.

The logic and rationale of moving in a new service direction must be demonstrated in the capital budgeting process so that the reviewers have a clear idea of the value, contribution, and viability of the projections. The greater and more viable the contribution, the more achievable a new service goal is and the more likely the capital expenditures will be approved.

Most capital expenditures have a specified format or planning system that nurse managers can use to frame their requests for purchases. These include the item,

Exhibit 7-2 Four-Year Capital Budget

D—CAPITAL BUDGET
FY 1987 thru 1990

Page 1 of 1

Responsibility Center:

Name: Nursing

Number: 987

Expend. Class	Rev.? Y or N	Qty.	Vendor	Item or Project Description	Cost by Year of Pay. or Proj. Comp.				Cost Source
					FY 1989	FY 1988	FY 1989	FY 1990	
B	N	1	IBM	Selectric Typewriter (replaces Underwood manual)			$1,000		V
E	N	1	Steelcase	Office Modular Furniture System		$15,000	$15,000	$20,000	E
				Totals	—	15,000	16,000	20,000	

Submitted By: E.F.

Admin. Review: L.B.

the quantity, the price, the manufacturer, the model name and number, and any other general or specific information.

The justification for the choices made should be presented, along with classifying it as to its profitability or its nonprofit-generating status. There also should be an indication whether it replaces existing equipment, fits in with the plan for growth, is a substitution for another resource, or is associated with new program plans (see Exercise 7-3). Along with the capital expense request should be a capital plan or pro forma statement on items that are revenue generating or income producing. When capital equipment generates revenue, that fact—and the anticipated amount—should be identified.

When the gross operating revenues from the use of capital equipment have been identified, the normal deductions relate to contractual adjustments (determined by payer relationship) and to the institution's provision for bad debt. The deductions should be summed and subtracted from the total gross operating revenue to produce the net operating revenue.

Next, items that relate to the cost of implementing the program associated with the capital purchase are identified. For instance, operating expenses include various payroll levels such as administration, staff, nursing, ancillary, and support services involved in delivering the care related to the purchase.

The operating cost of the equipment itself must be determined and added to the expense items associated with the capital purchase. Depreciation is of concern. It represents the decline in value of capital equipment because of the wear and tear of normal use as well as obsolescence. It usually is measured in yearly increments through charging a portion of the asset (the equipment's value) and its original cost against the income it produces.

If rental of equipment is involved, it must be identified as a part of the cost of doing business. Any interest accruing as a part of a long-term purchase of a capital item or other purchases should be included in the income account.

If appropriate, amortization should be included. Amortization is an accounting technique similar to depreciation that involves charging off the cost of certain assets (usually intangibles such as patents and copyrights) in the capital plan over a defined number of years. Amortization and other service cost items should be included in the operating expense portion of the pro forma statement outlining the capital plan.

When all operating expenses have been identified, they are added to give the total operating expense for a capital plan. That total is subtracted from the net operating revenue, leaving net operating income. This measures the viability of the capital purchase process (see Exercise 7-4).

CAPITAL REIMBURSEMENT

The financing process for capital purchases in health care changed in the mid-1980s. Most such purchases in the past had been supported through the reimbursement program. Since the change from cost-based reimbursement to prospective payment system (PPS), capital costs have been paid as they had been traditionally in the cost-based system. Under prospective pricing, some newer strategy is involved.

One national issue is: What percent (if any) of an institution's capitalization should be assumed by federal payers? The percent of capital reimbursement or payment is important in determining the essential value of the capital payment portion under the prospective pricing structure. Since an institution's ability to capitalize for operation and growth is essential to its success, the capital payment process has a dramatic impact on every health care facility.

Meanwhile, the nurse manager must be very careful in her planning. As institutions become more cost conscious, as inpatient revenues decline, and as the PPS continues to stabilize, much less revenue will be available for capital planning. Capital budgeting processes are being reviewed and each request is being scrutinized for its value to the institution and its viability.

CAPITAL AND CASH REVISITED

Capital budget planning is centered on "what-if" questions that are difficult to answer since they involve large sums of money over long periods of time.

Perhaps the simplest method of justifying a capital expenditure is the payback approach. This is built on the belief that a capital expenditure will pay for itself from its operating savings over a defined number of years. For example, two capital expenditures are identified as Item #1 and Item #2, both costing $25,000 and both of which will return savings in operations to pay for themselves in a specified number of years—five in this instance.

Under a payback approach any direct method of payment would be equally desirable because it would meet the management goal as to length of repayment. The shorter the payback time the better. In the payback approach, the manager evaluates how long it will be before receipts on the investment equal the amount of money invested. Item #1 can continue in operation for several years beyond that point, producing savings in that extra time. Item #2 meanwhile has ceased functioning before the fifth year, ending its value to the institution.

One of the justifications for a capital expenditure is the rate of return that results from the revenue it produces. In this case, a number of approaches can be employed. An asset can be identified at its gross value or at its net value after depreciation. This may include leased or rented assets or can be restricted to items in which the institution holds ownership.

It may not make any real difference which of the two methods is used. Both have serious limitations in that they do not consider the time value of money. The two competing capital feasibility processes can be expected to result in the same rate of return. However, one again may produce value earlier in the life of the capital plan, and the other later. Earlier production of value, if all other variables are equal, is generally a better investment because the earlier, higher receipts can be invested in interest-bearing accounts. Under the rate-of-return method, both may be equally beneficial, whereas other techniques could produce different outcomes.

An institution or service can be profitable to the extent that it has net income. Profitability can be enhanced by the investment strategy undertaken. Since a dollar earned today has more value than one in the future, it should be apparent to the nurse manager that the value of a dollar is reflected in the time frame in which it is used. It is because of this time value of money that interest becomes an issue and the net value of the money becomes important.

The net present value analysis approach indicates that there is a specific minimum rate that is acceptable to the institution. The goal of this approach is to determine whether a capital project will actually earn the desired or required rate of return. Applying this required rate to all expected future cash flows (the financial office has tables for accomplishing this) will result in an outcome in which the present value can be compared with the amount of proposed capital expenditure over time. If a present value equals or exceeds capital funding, an expenditure can be deemed appropriate.

Capital expenditures usually increase because they accompany other changes in the institution: higher personnel costs, new services, new plans. Because capital projects also cost money, the timing of investment in them should be related to forecasts of an increase in the nursing service.

A number of approaches can be used in looking at the cash values associated with capital planning and recognizing that it is an investment in the future of the institution. As such, the investment nature of the capital process, such as the time value of money, must receive serious consideration.

In capital planning, the use of cash for purchasing equipment must be reviewed by the financial officer and the nurse manager to determine the best approaches to such an outlay. In this way, the capital planning and purchasing process can be structured on the basis of the needs of the institution, the cost of the capital plan, its components and uses, its return on capital, and its impact on cash.

The nurse manager is a central player in this process. She therefore must have a basic understanding of capital management and planning. Capital planning that fits within the organization's plan makes a real contribution to the health care institution.

Here again, data bases, historical information, the ability to forecast, and the use of skills to project marketing and service needs all come together in a nursing systems context to provide the nurse manager with tools to make decisions (see Exercise 7-5). When a good nursing capital planning system is in place, the institution and the services it offers are enhanced; when a capital planning process is missing, the facility pays a price. Without a well-prepared nurse manager to drive this process, the institution is disadvantaged.

In summary it should be clear to the nurse manager that logical and consistent formats in designing capital plans operate much the same way as any objective-setting process. The mechanics may be different, but the process is the same. Adequate data, assessment of the data, determination of value, forecasting, developing operational and capital plans, evaluating their possibilities, and structuring the cost framework are central to the management role in any clinical service.

SUGGESTED READINGS

American Institute Of Certified Public Accountants. *Statement On Auditing Standards,* 1973.

Horngren, Charles. *Accounting for Management Control:* An Introduction. Englewood Cliffs, N.J.: Prentice-Hall, Inc., 1974, 421–423.

Neuschel, Richard. *Management for Profit And Growth.* New York: McGraw-Hill Publishing Co., 1976.

Appendix 7-A

Exercise and Practice Tools

Exercise 7-1 Capital Budget

Responsibility Center:

Name: _____

Number: _____

Clinical: _____

Nonclinical: _____

Page _____ of _____

C—CAPITAL BUDGET
FY 198___-8___

Expend. Class	Rev.? Y or N	Qty.	Vendor	Item or Project Description	Mo. of Order	Total Cost by Pay. or Proj. Comp. Date			Cost Source	Maint. Agree.
						4/8 – 9/8	10/8 – 3/8	Aft 3/8		
					Totals					

Submitted By: _____   Reviewed By: _____

Exercise 7-2 Four-Year Capital Budget

C—CAPITAL BUDGET
FY 198 __8__

Responsibility Center: _____

Name: _____ _____

Number: _____

Page _____ of _____

Expend. Class	Rev.? Y or N	Qty.	Vendor	Item or Project Description	Cost by Year of Pay. or Proj. Comp.				Cost Source
					FY 1987	FY 1988	FY 1989	FY 1990	
				Totals					

Submitted By: _____

Admin. Review: _____

Exercise 7-3 Capital Plan Form

FORM C-1
FY 198___ Capital Plan

1. Department	Cost Center	Revenue Center

2. Item Requested and Quantity

3. Manufacturer	4. Model Number

5. Additional Information

6. Total Estimated Cost	(A) Base Price_____
	(B) Freight_____
	(C) Installation_____
	(D) Other_____

Asset Life: Years:

7. Justification (Reason for Expenditure)

8. Expenditure Revenue Nonrevenue	9. Estimated Annual Profit
Classification Generating Generating	(see PRO FORMA)
(A) Accreditation/Licensure/	(A) Estimated Annual Total
Code Compliance	Add to Operating Income $
(B) Replacement	(B) Est. Annual Operation
	Cost, Including
(C) Growth	Maint. or Serv.
	Agreement $_____
(D) Resource Substitution	
(E) New Program	

10. Approvals

(A) Department Head	(D) Administrator
(B) Vice President for Nursing	(E) Executive Committee
(C) Vice President for Finance	(F) Board

Exercise 7-4 Pro Forma Operating Income Statement

PRO FORMA INCOME STATEMENT
198___ Capital Plan

Computation of Annual Contribution to Operating Income

	Total	
A. Section I		
Gross Operating Revenue:	$	%
Inpatient	_____	
Outpatient	_____	
Other Income	_____	
Total	_____	100%
Revenue Deductions		
Contractual Adjustment	_____	
Bad Debt Provision	_____	
Total	_____	
Net Operating Revenue	_____	
B. Section II		
Operating Expenses:		
Payroll—Administration & General	_____	
Payroll—Nursing & Ancillary	_____	
Payroll—Support Services	_____	
Total Payroll	_____	_____
Operating Cost	_____	_____
Depreciation	_____	_____
Rental—Real Estate & Equipment	_____	_____
Interest	_____	_____
Amortization	_____	_____
Total Operating Expenses	_____	_____
Net Operating Income	_____	_____

	Assumed Cost-Based Reimb.	%	Assumed Charge-Based Reim.	%	Total	
Inpatient	_____	%	_____	%		
Outpatient	_____	%	_____	%	_____	%
	_____	%	_____	%	_____	%

Exercise 7-5   Statement of Budget Problem and Solution

PROBLEM AND SOLUTION STATEMENT
Capital Budget Plan

Project Title_____ Accountable Manager_____

Problem Statement

1. Describe the problem:

2. Identify medical and hospital staff members who have helped define the problem:

Exercise 7-5 continued
Solution Statement
1. Describe briefly the proposed solution to the problem:

2. Discuss how the proposed project will resolve the problem:

3. Identify available alternative solutions, and why they were rejected:

4. Describe the standard uses associated with the project:

_____   _____

Signature (of person completing form)   Date

Budget Control and Negotiation

OBJECTIVES FOR CHAPTER 8

This chapter will:
1. *Discuss the involvement of nursing staff in the budget planning process.*
2. *Identify processes the nurse manager can utilize in expanding the roles of all members of the nursing care team in budget planning.*
3. *Review some of the problems of managing in the real world while maintaining an appropriate budget framework.*
4. *Outline management processes essential to ensure success in the budget control and evaluation components of the financial plan.*
5. *Define relevant operational variances and their control essential to the nurse manager.*
6. *Identify elements of finalizing and defending a unit or department financial plan.*
7. *Outline characteristics of the health care organization of the 21st century and the nurse manager's role in preparing for the future.*

No budget planning can have any meaning if the nurse manager is not able to operate successfully within the budget. A budget plan provides an opportunity for her to define her organization in financial terms. However, after this process has been completed successfully, it is her obligation to operate her service or department well within those financial limits.

If the planning has been careful and appropriate time has been spent in preparation, operating within the plan should be a relatively straightforward process. However, when planning has not been as thorough as it could be, variances have been significant. In the author's experience, nurse managers have had many variances, in most cases the result of inadequate planning, inappropriate negotiating during the budget process, or the inability to use a systematic and consistent approach to operating the budget during the year.

Here again, planning and management systems take on importance. If appropriate systems are in place that the nurse manager can use in making decisions, her management of the budget should be relatively simple. If patient classification and acuity measures are used, staffing for the delivery of care should be structured clearly to provide the nurse manager with needed information. If she has a monitoring method that evaluates the patient in the context of the DRG classification or nursing diagnostic classification, she can determine the costs of providing care; she then can balance that figure against the total cost provided for that patient in the context of the classification.

Such strategies and control mechanisms help the nurse manager deal with patient-specific items that may be at variance with the budget plan. The important point is that the institutions have a mechanism to enable the manager to respond as quickly as possible to correct errors or variances.

INVOLVEMENT OF STAFF MEMBERS

Everyone in the nursing organization should have some familiarity with the financial and budgeting process. As with most processes, the staff members who carry out the nursing objectives (including budgetary) should be involved in their formulation. This way, when the performance requirements and constraints have been identified in the planning process, the staff members are familiar with the expectations they generate. Management and staff together address the planning and operating issues (goals, plans, programs, capital operations, and control) through their ongoing work, as evidenced by their commitment (investment), understanding of the issues (identification), and willingness to work together (participation) to achieve outcomes (see Figure 8-1).

When staff members are involved in financial processes, they are aware of the limitations and can cooperate more effectively. Their understanding that there are cost constraints on every activity in the department helps them realize that all behavior must conform to those resources.

The nurse manager therefore must incorporate into her operating behavior options and opportunities for staff involvement. For example, she might:

- Assign an individual staff member to review the specifics of the patient classification system for any given day when nursing care is provided. Correlating the patient classification or acuity indexes with the staffing levels for the day, noting any variance from the plan, helps the nurses recognize and buy into the process of controlling staffing costs.

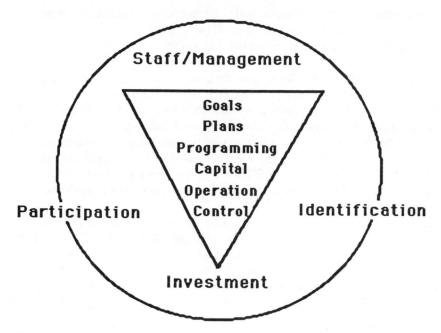

Figure 8-1 Staff Responsibility in Financial Planning and Control

- Work with the financial office to devise a cost format for determining the costs to date for every patient receiving nursing services. This helps the nursing staff recognize the cost factors involved in providing care. A comparison of a particular patient's daily costs and summary cost to date with the total cost allocated for the care of that client gives the staff members a view of their activities, their costs, and how effectively the nurses are functioning.
- Review patient classification, supply, and material costs and variances at the monthly nursing staff meeting. This incorporates costs as a part of the unit deliberations on activities affecting its operation.
- Review specific cost variances periodically with individual nurses to help them understand the issues and to get their input as to possible strategies to reduce the variances.
- Include the nursing staff in the budget planning process, even in completion of certain portions of the budget. Nurses who look at staffing, material and supply, and program costs acquire a more realistic picture of the processes and the situation.

The budgeting process should not be a painful experience. Most everyone, in order to provide opportunities for motivation and growth, sets personal goals that they strive to achieve. Similarly, the budgeting process provides opportunities for the nursing organization to set specific goals that it seeks to achieve. Identifying, then structuring, a financial plan that will support those goals is the cornerstone of the budgeting process. Monitoring and controlling such a budget becomes merely a review of performance against the goals.

The real problem for the nurse manager is attempting to involve the nursing staff in controlling the implementation of the budget and in noting variances. One reason is that traditionally budget control was regarded as managerial, not clinical, work. When a nursing organization is structured to meet mutually defined goals, this separation of management and clinical roles is less important. This is as it should be in meeting particular clinical goals. Those involved in achieving these goals have some obligation to assure that this is done in a mutually acceptable manner.

Therefore, the management team must be cooperative in its attitude toward those processes. Since the team has been inculcated with the belief that it is its responsibility both to plan and to control financial resources, any other mechanism generally is not considered appropriate by administration or by staff. However, the true professional character of nursing relationships involves a sharing or mutuality of obligation in financial planning just as in the clinical delivery of care.

RESTRUCTURING THE PROCESS

Since the financial plan is merely a numeric interpretation of the processes associated with delivering care, it would seem appropriate that all those involved in the delivery of care should participate in the processes that plan the costs and payment associated with that patient service. Under such circumstances, the management process must be structured differently. The budget plan no longer should be the concern of the nurse manager alone; it should involve all the nursing staff. Management at the various levels should expect that the mechanics of planning, controlling, and operating the budget are the obligation of the entire care delivery team. Each member has an impact and should have input (see Figure 8-2).

It is important to have accurate information in terms that are clear enough that nursing staff members understand what is expected of them. The nurse manager's asking them to police costs without explaining which ones need to be controlled and the best mechanisms for doing so is not the way to instill accountability.

When specific costs must be controlled, they should be identified in terms of the budget limits and of potential variances. A variance is simply a difference from what was planned. If there is a difference, there must be a reason for it. Ascertaining the reason may lead the nursing staff to discover problems in the

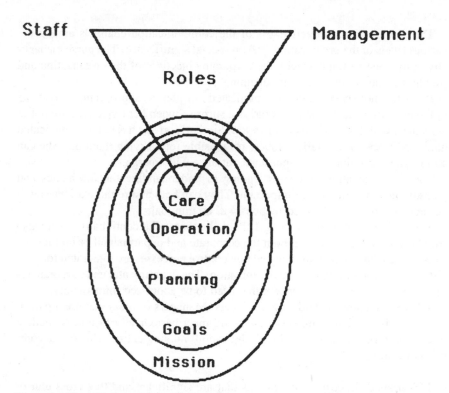

Figure 8-2 Shared Relationship In Goal Achievement

delivery of services or even with the initial plan. All of the factors having an impact on a variance should be understood by the staff, and a step-by-step mechanism provided for correcting it.

Variances (and other circumstances) can necessitate alterations not anticipated at the outset of the financial planning. The important point is not that there is variance but that it be understood and that corrective steps be incorporated into the planning structure. Here again, the nursing staff must have concrete information about the variance, and be able to participate in planning for adjusting it. The more involvement the nursing staff has in that process, the better and more effectively variance adjustments can be dealt with.

An additional benefit to the nurse manager is that she is better informed and better supported in variance analysis and in control of the budget plan. When her administrator asks the nurse manager to account for a significant budget variance, she should use every staff resource having information. This can help assure the administrator that the manager has both an understanding of and a legitimate response to the variance.

The timeliness and effectiveness of the communication channels among the various levels of the organization take on special significance. The nurse manager obviously must be familiar with the corporate objectives of the organization and should incorporate them into her planning.

If she has not successfully communicated her plan to appropriate individuals in the institution, it should not come as a surprise when her objectives are not in agreement with those of the organization. Similarly, if she has not communicated goals and plans to the staff members responsible for carrying them out, she can almost guarantee that some significant variance will emerge.

The communication processes leading to understanding the mechanics and goals of budget planning are important. They can help assure that variances will be limited and the need for corrections will be minimal.

The implementation of the budget should be monitored continually. There also should be periodic reviews at both the corporate and departmental or unit levels. This assures that the institutional and unit control processes are integrated for consistent operation throughout the organization. The departmental and corporate review can identify areas of concern that need to be addressed immediately.

These evaluations should be at all levels. Managers of units that are a part of a large division of nursing services should meet periodically to discuss budget issues and problems associated with the overall nursing entity. This can accomplish two things:

1. Variances in costs or operations that are significant and that cross unit or departmental levels can be identified, and recommendations for corrections can be made.
2. Nurse managers can support each other in the learning and developmental processes associated with budget control and can work collectively in responding to variances identified at the unit level.

Where there are systems problems, nurse managers together can develop strategies to correct the difficulties, thus having an impact on the cost of doing business (see Figure 8-3).

VARIANCE PROCESSES

Variances at the corporate level are composed of small anomalies at lower levels that, when aggregated, can involve significant dollars. For instance, if a number of departments have overutilized materials and supplies, the total can be sizable. Since variance analysis is based on the contributions of each individual unit to the aggregate, it is important that even small differences be noted so that adjustments can be made to reduce the impact on the institution.

Figure 8-3 Role Integration in the Finance Process

An important consideration for the nursing service is that it constitutes a large portion of the institution's financial resources committed to care. In that context, any variance in nursing can create a significant difference in the institution. As a result, the nursing services have a special obligation to be cognizant of their unique contribution to the overall cost framework. Variance analysis in nursing thus takes on special importance. If the total accrued variance in one service over a specific period is $100,000 and there are ten such services in the nursing organization, a single unit of accrual could become an aggregate of $1 million. That would have a tremendous impact on the organization, so the department's ability to conduct variance analysis and quick corrective action are vital to the success of the institution.

One important consideration in variance analysis is the ability to identify the anomaly at the lowest unit level. If item budgeting is sufficiently detailed so that individual units of service can be identified and costed, then it is easier to find the variance. However, when unit costs are aggregated with others and so classified and budgeted, it will be more difficult to identify the problem. The larger the unit of cost, the more difficult it is to account for it, and, of course, vice versa.

Therefore, in budget planning, the nurse manager should work with the finance office to account for individual expense items that relate to the operation of her service. It should be easy to track and monitor such items. Since operating reports must be received at regular intervals, the nurse manager can act quickly to correct significant variances.

The finance office must maintain data on a multitude of services and financial circumstances. Such data are not always accessible for variance analysis by individual departments; indeed, sometimes they are not included in the financial office monthly operating reports. However, some flexibility usually can be built into the reporting mechanism that can be used to provide information specific to individual entities below the top level. If the nursing division needs unique processes or information by department or unit, those sometimes can be incorporated into the monthly report. Where that cannot be done, the nurse manager must devise internal reporting mechanisms to meet her needs.

The reports she needs generally should reflect the character and functions of the operation and the nursing unit or service: data essential to sound operating processes, the value of the data in terms of variance analysis, and the viability of the action taken in response.

It is necessary to remind the nurse manager that data collection for the sake of data collection is of little value and can waste energy and time. She must recognize which data are important and develop mechanisms to monitor and analyze them. Which processes need such monitoring is purely her judgment.

It is wiser to look at items with the possibility of a wide range of variance; where there is limited possibility of variance, detailed monitoring may not be as necessary.

CORRECTIVE RESPONSES

When a variance is detected, the nurse manager must begin corrective responses. It may be best to monitor variances over the shortest period possible for quicker adjustment. For example, with a staffing variance, the nurse manager should be obtaining data on unit staffing on a daily basis. A pattern of variance then should become clear in a short period such as a week.

The unit's circumstances will indicate the best corrective response to an item that is extremely cost sensitive. The nurse manager may find that tracking stock materials and supplies on an individual service or unit is even more difficult to monitor in a brief time. Sufficient time must pass for a pattern to emerge so she can base the corrective steps on reasonably accurate data.

Sometimes, the response to what the data reveal may be more important than the length of time it takes to collect the information. For example, a given month may show an extreme variance in supply usage even though there is limited variance in any of the areas affecting supply usage. Since the month in which the variance occurred already has passed and the data indicating whether corrective action has been successful will not be available for another month, the nurse manager essentially has a window of two months before the adjustments can show results. Therefore, immediate response is essential to capture that time lost between the discovery of the variance and the corrective measures. Even so, in this case immediate action still can put the nurse manager a month behind in returning to the budgeted standard.

The nurse manager should identify the fastest ways to detect variances. However, when investigating variances with the nursing staff, she must be careful to avoid potentially erroneous assumptions and seek to get to the real source of the problem. Changes in patient population, intensity, or acuity might be blamed but the nurse manager must have supporting data to be sure. Where there clearly has been overutilization of resources, she has a strong indication that there is at least a limited relationship.

The prospective payment structure under which most hospital services now are being paid puts pressure on the nurse manager to isolate variances and remedy them. Here again, she should use the staff's skills to help assess the patterns that could cause the anomaly.

ON THE DOWNSIDE

On the downside of budget planning is the accelerated rate of change in health care. Regardless of how careful and how thorough the planning process is, variances always should be anticipated. Social, structural, environmental, and systems changes are inevitable, influence the rules for managing, and alter anticipated outcomes. Because health care is in a human-intensive service environment, many variables associated with its management can change radically what nurses do. As a result, any number of circumstances may be altered by factors beyond the nurse manager's control. She thus must learn to live in an environment that is constantly in change, which means that variances must be expected.

One of the goals of good planning is to keep the negative impact of variances from having a significant effect on the organization. When a variance occurs that clearly is beyond the control of the service, responsive alternatives—such as readjusting the budget, changing service goals, or altering staffing levels—must be available to the manager. Overreacting or underreacting can aggravate the situation. Careful analysis, appropriate adjustments, and accommodations that fit the circumstances are the best responses.

The nurse manager can expect to see numerous kinds of variances that singly or collectively create the problem. Her ability to recognize those factors can help her get at the source.

One of the most common problems involves what is called the rate or price variance. This occurs when the department spends more per unit than had been budgeted. In nursing, this often is related to salary adjustments. Because of the swings between surplus and dearth of nurses, salary changes are frequent. These can include cost-of-living raises, changes to reflect market conditions, merit increases, bonuses, etc. The term price variance usually stems from changes by vendors. The budget then must be adjusted to the new prices.

The amount of services can be higher or lower than budgeted. This is a volume variance and is caused simply by the fact that the resource has been used either more or less than anticipated. This can affect staffing and utilization of materials, supplies, and personnel.

However, there are some extenuating circumstances. If there is an increase in volume but not in intensity, the utilization of nursing resources may be stable or reduced; with a decrease in volume but an increase in related intensity, the adjustment in resource use should reflect that situation. The nurse manager again must be able to identify those factors so she may understand their impact on her operation.

A third problem is the use variance. This is simply the use of more resources per unit of service than was planned. This is the most common variance in nursing. The nurse manager must determine whether that resource use is appropriate or whether the planned requirement was insufficient for the workload that developed. Any discrepancies must be resolved by the nurse manager, either by insisting on reduced utilization of resources or by increasing the amount projected in the planning process.

The use of more resources than planned when there is no change in volume can become a serious concern. Those responsible for budget planning may not be aware of the factors that have led to this situation. They should be informed promptly so they can take the reasons into consideration in the next round of budgeting.

The next factor is exception reporting. This is an organized process in which the nurse manager reports to administration all variances, their source, the reason for them, and adjustments or justification as appropriate. If the exception reports involve major problems, they usually are incorporated into the organization's financial planning and evaluation process and serve as a base for adjustments. Exception reporting is especially important in a division as large as nursing. Exception reports generally are submitted for the institution's regular monthly operating financial review.

As costs become even more controlled as health care institutions move to the 21st century, the ability to implement flexible budgeting processes and variance analysis and control will be key to the success of the nurse manager. As noted, she essentially is a businesswoman in charge of a business enterprise. She must realize that certain skills and mechanics in the financial planning process are central to her success: the ability to plan, implement, control, and evaluate a specific program consistent with the goals and objectives of the service and the organization as a whole. To the extent that she does so, the organization is enhanced and the service is made more viable. Therefore, it behooves the nurse manager to obtain as much information, support, and resources as possible in undertaking an effective financial planning process through developing academic and practical skills.

FINALIZING THE BUDGET PLAN

When the nurse manager has completed the budget planning process, she submits it for incorporation into the institution's budget. She must remember that she is competing for funds and resources in an institution that offers a variety of services. As those resources become more tightly controlled and less generally available, the nurse manager will recognize that there are limitations on their availability.

Each of the organization's programs must have some meaning or value for the institution as a whole. Much of the nurse manager's progress and success will depend on her ability to defend and promote nursing services, the facility's need for them, and their value to the organization as a whole.

Budget planning need not be a traumatic experience. If all of the pieces of the process are in place and have been designed appropriately, the nurse manager should feel confident that she is prepared for the negotiation processes with administration. If she has reviewed her data base, if her analysis and assessment of the marketplace is correct and can be validated, and if the design of her budget plan is well integrated, clearly justified, and appropriate to the needs of the service, her proposals should be approved with little or no change because she will have proved their value to the institution.

The wise nurse manager recognizes that the more she can tie her budget into the overall goals and objectives of the institution, the more likely it will be approved. This means she must present evidence of the close relationship—the synergy—involving her budget plan and that of the organization.

The budget officers' time for conducting the review process obviously has finite limits so the manager must learn to make her presentation clear, precise, and succinct, yet at the same time get across the message as to the value of her service.

BUDGET PLAN REVIEW

In preparing for review of her budget plan, the nurse manager should:

1. Make sure that priorities are established clearly, identified succinctly, listed in order of value, and their cost and resource utilization identifiable. Where the production of income is a major consideration, the revenue projection should be as specific as possible. Identified expenses should be related to the income and be well within the cost parameters as a percent of revenue as determined by the institution.
2. Justify the capital plan within the context of the service provided. Capital items should be presented in relation to the service to be provided and should be reasonable.
3. Anticipate the questions that the budget review panel will ask. She should know her facts and figures, anticipate conflict points, recognize that the members of the panel have their own agendas, and make her argument logical.
4. Defend but not retrench. The nurse manager should make her points and try to avoid prolonged arguing or debating the viability of the plan with individual members of the panel. She is presenting what she believes to be the best possible mix of strategies for implementing a successful budget plan for her service. She should make the presentation clear, defend it logically, and attempt to maintain a positive attitude.
5. Respond to questions that require follow-up, change, or reallocation of resources, accept adjustments that the panel insists on, follow through where she or the panel still have questions, and, again, maintain a positive attitude. If the nurse manager has any further questions or concerns as to requested adjustments, she should follow them through with the administrator, obtain advice, then resubmit them as appropriate.

The nurse manager should recognize that the objective of the budget review committee is to stay within the cost limits established in the annual or periodic financial plan and will look at nursing's proposal in that context. It obviously always seeks to save costs where possible so it will attempt to identify such points in the nurse manager's plan.

The budget review committee is not composed of ogres and usually is willing to try to be accommodating within the constraints under which it operates. Where it is determined that costs need minor adjustments, the nurse manager should work with her administrator to do so. If, on the other hand, the panel requires significant adjustments and the nurse manager cannot negotiate an easing in its position, she must work out the situation with her administrator and resubmit the plan when it is within the required parameters.

The budget review process can be an emotionally demanding experience. The manager who has committed a great deal of time, energy, and resources to developing a sound and meaningful plan enters the session with the hope that the committee will accept her recommendations. Unfortunately she often will leave the meeting disappointed and discouraged because she feels the review process does not appear to do justice to, or have a sufficient commitment to, her plan. She must be prepared for this.

The budget review committee must look at the plan in an objective way and determine its fit with the corporate goals. It does not, and cannot, have the same investment and involvement in the plan as has the nurse manager. She must recognize the limitations of the budget review process and draw support from the belief that she has committed her resources and energy to design the best possible proposal under the circumstances.

Here again, she should seek support in communication with her peers and with her administrator, and together they should share their feelings, frustrations, and satisfactions, providing mutual backing.

PREPARING FOR THE 21ST CENTURY

Throughout these chapters, the cornerstone of the budget planning process has been preparation and the generation of data upon which sound decisions can be made. The decisionmaking and budget planning processes depend on a systematic development and assessment of data, utilization of projection and forecasting tools, and an effective control and monitoring system.

The nurse manager who has developed these tools and has used them consistently in her budget planning can feel confident that she has followed the best possible approach and that her plan will be consistent with the institution's goals, will be viable, and will be acceptable to the organization as a whole. From that acceptance, she can move with confidence into operating her service or unit so as to meet the objectives that she has established for providing nursing services to a demanding patient population.

As with any organization, there is no substitute for good management and good planning. The nurse manager who plans her organizational needs, manages them within the limits provided, and assesses, controls, adjusts, and evaluates her operation consistent with the institution's overall approach can be assured that her service not only will be meaningful and viable but also will be successful.

This text has focused on the planning of financial resources within the context of a changing health care system. The program approach has been emphasized as the key in the financial planning process. It is important to emphasize the value inherent in such an approach.

Nurses of the future will be practicing in places and in ways tremendously different from those of the past. The new health care setting will demand skills and relationships well beyond the performance expectations of most nurses up to this point. It is assumed that as the health care system continues its transition to this setting that many new approaches to service provision will be developed.

Perhaps 60 percent of the health care services will be offered in settings away from acute care hospitals. These service centers will be decentralized and often will have their own small service groups that will be fully responsible for the activities there. The centers will generate their own full range of activities. Nurses not only will staff but also will manage many of these centers. They will be responsible for the full range of activities associated with marketing, planning, operating, and evaluating the work offered in such settings. Thus, they obviously will need new sets of skills if they are to be successful in this work environment.

The corporate structure will be rearranged to assure the marketability, manageability, and success of the multilevel health services system (see Figure 8-4). Nursing as a corporate division or structure will have broader accountability for the services provided, including their planning and control. Competitiveness will increase and have a greater impact on how corporate fiscal resources are divided. Those who can show their viability in service and dollars will win corporate support.

The development of skills in fiscal management and control will be essential to nursing success. The nurse manager must continue to develop in these areas in order to provide the new kind of leadership. Financial aspects will be stressed

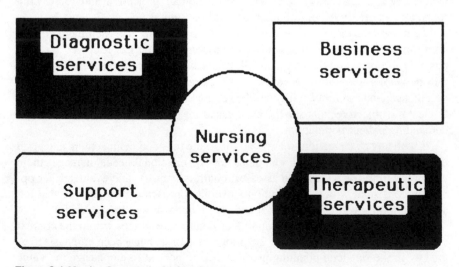

Figure 8-4 Nursing Structure in the 21st Century

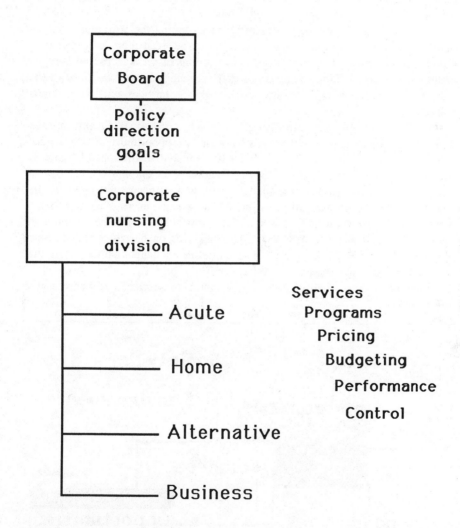

Figure 8-5 Corporate Nursing Structural Format

even more in setting goals for both the institution and nursing, defined in terms of dollars, margins, levels of profitability, and growth. How services achieve those goals, the mechanisms for offering services, the roles assumed, and the staff mix will be internal considerations (see Figure 8-5).

Nurses will have much more flexibility in designing the workplace, subject of course to costs. Pricing of services will become even more important than now because of the stiff competition. If institutions or services cannot compete in the price market, failure is guaranteed. Everyone must be sensitized to that reality. Well-defined, high-quality, price-sensitive services will be the most marketable.

It should be evident that many changes will be occurring in the health care system. The ability to anticipate them provides the best opportunity to offer leadership in coping with them. Nursing must be prepared to offer a full range of responses to such changes. However, anticipation is not enough.

Leadership in the marketplace of the future will demand a set of skills that evidence the ability to plan, forecast, price, and execute nursing and health care services in a wide variety of contexts. The nurse manager will be on the front lines of this new health care system. The demands on her role will increase. She must develop skills necessary for meeting this challenge. To the extent that she has the skills, the energy, and the creativity to provide this new leadership, the outcome will be quality, diversity, richness of service, and success (see Figure 8-6).

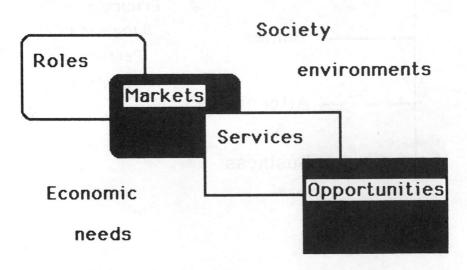

Figure 8-6 External/Internal Nursing Service Interface

SUGGESTED READINGS

American College of Health Care Executives. *Health Care in the 1990s: Trends and Strategy*. New York: Arthur Andersen & Co. 1984.

Anthony, Robert, and David Young. *Management Control in Nonprofit Organizations*. Homewood, Ill.: Richard D. Irwin, Inc., 1984, 233–590.

Gross, Malvern. *Financial and Accounting Guide for Nonprofit Organizations*. New York: The Ronald Press Company, 1983.

Kaiser, Leland. "Future Plan," *Group Practice Journal* (May-June 1984): 54–68.

Sheldon, Alan, and Susan Windham. *Competitive Strategy for Health Care Organizations*. New York: Dow Jones-Irwin, 1984.

Financial Planning Framework, Instructions, and Practice Tools[*]

This is based on an actual program. Some of the elements discussed may not be available in all institutions. In such cases, appropriate suggestions can be made to the Finance Division on including or adapting helpful items.

---

[*]Special thanks to Len Bryant, vice president of finance, St. Joseph's Hospital, Atlanta, for his role in preparing the material in this Appendix.

Fiscal Year 198__ to 198__ Budget
General and Detailed Instructions

CONTENTS

Budget Calendar

General Instructions:

Detailed Instructions:

Practice Forms

REVISED BUDGET CALENDAR

December 29, 198___	Circulate instructions, forms, and data to departments.
January 6, 198___	Conduct first training and help session.
January 9, 198___	Meet to review patient day forecasts. Review assumptions with Senior Staff.
January 10, 198___	Conduct TEAM[1] orientation session.
January 19, 198___	Review process and assumptions with Finance Committee.
January 20, 198___	Last date for return of all data to Finance Office.
January 24, 198___	Capital input to TEAM.
January 26, 198___	Finish edits and system inputs.
January 27, 198___	Return printouts to departments.
January 31, 198___	Last date for corrections to Finance Office.
February 3, 198___	Review of new programs and services.
February 7, 198___	Vice President for Finance and President review of budget.
February 8–10, 198___	Budget hearings. Completion of TEAM.
February 14, 198___	Budget Committee meeting on capital. Completion of cash budget. Completion of forecasts and financial modeling.
February 16, 198___	Presentation to Finance Committee.
February 23, 198___	Possible presentation to Executive Committee.
March 10, 198___	Financial presentation to Board. Three-year capital plan to SHPDA.[2]

---

1. TEAM = Technology Evaluation and Acquisition Methods (for hospitals).
2. SHPDA = State Health Planning and Development Agency.

I. OVERVIEW

Each year, management prepares budgets for the coming fiscal year. Budgets are necessary for the planning and management of the health care institution and are required by accrediting and monitoring agencies.

A budget may be defined simply as "a plan expressed in dollars." As such, the plan must incorporate goals and objectives necessary to achieve the mission, short-range, and long-range plans of the hospital. Such plans then are translated into dollar terms. The overall budget is compiled from departmental budgets and therefore serves as a vehicle to quantify the financial requirements and expected results from all levels of operation.

The completed budget, whether at the departmental level or for the entire facility, provides a means of reviewing past decisions and making future decisions on:

- plans for departments
- plans for the institution
- financial ability to complete plans
- necessity of modifying plans
- making capital expenditures
- setting rates and charges to patients
- allocating operating resources.

Thorough and accurate budgeting will provide a description of and monitor for the conduct of the institution's business and will prevent unexpected financial demands from hindering progress toward completing planned activities.

II. HIGHLIGHTS OF THE FY 198__–8__ BUDGET

The highlights of the budgeting process this year are:

- Budget forms will be distributed and collected as a package. All forms will go out and must be returned as a set.
- An opportunity will be provided for new responsibility centers to be created as a means for describing operations of previously combined (bundled) departments more discretely (see Section IV for more detail).
- An opportunity is provided to create natural accounts in the operating expense portion as a means of describing expenses generically by type rather than system and providing more exact definitions of expenses.

- A Chart of Accounts has been developed to make available to managers a wide range of both old and new expense categories and to provide standardized definitions of each expense type.
- Standard forms have been provided to detail expenses using a zero-base methodology where appropriate.
- Salary and Wage budgets will be compiled for 26 pay periods rather than 12 months to facilitate analysis of variances throughout the coming year.
- Capital Expenditure budgets will be developed in two components: (1) a detailed budget for FY 198__–8__, and (2) a general forecast for 198__ through 198__.
- Data Processing support will use in-house equipment and systems.
- Detailed instructions have been provided for each form.

III. GENERAL INSTRUCTIONS

1. Please write neatly using #2 pencil for all numeric entries throughout the budget formset. Narrative information may be typed or written in ink.
2. Read instructions thoroughly before completing each section.
3. Plan to attend the training and help and TEAM orientation sessions noted on the calendar. Notices will be circulated before each session.
4. Call the Finance office for assistance whenever necessary.
5. Throw away any work sheets that do not apply to your responsibility center.
6. Use N/A for "not applicable" in any work sheet fields for which no entry is appropriate.
7. Extra work sheet copies will be available from the Finance office.
8. Do not copy work sheets until all entries are complete and initial review has been made by the Finance staff.
9. Be sure to check all items on the checklist under "Returned" (or use N/A) as an inventory before submitting the folder for initial review by the Finance staff.
10. Use whole dollars except for spread factors (factor by which indicated items are multiplied). Use up to three decimal places for spread factors.

IV. NEW RESPONSIBILITY CENTERS AND CHART OF ACCOUNTS

The FY 198__–8__ budget process provides the opportunity to create new responsibility centers and defines expense accounts.

The steps are necessary in order to break out large organizational units into small, discrete management entities so that financial results can be measured and controlled in more detail. If the institution currently has numerous functions bundled together into relatively few cost centers, that practice will require change.

IF YOU FEEL YOU HAVE THE NEED TO CREATE NEW, UN-BUNDLED RESPONSIBILITY CENTERS, READ APPENDIX A-1 TO THESE INSTRUCTIONS.

CREATION OF A NEW RESPONSIBILITY CENTER WILL RE-QUIRE A NEW NUMBER AND A SEPARATE FORM SET FOR THE FY 198__–8__ BUDGET.

Appendix 1 also discusses the "natural" classification of expenses. Expenses have been redefined for FY 198__–8__ in the Chart of Accounts (Appendix A-2 of these instructions).

BE SURE TO READ APPENDIX A-2 BEFORE ATTEMPTING TO
COMPLETE THE OPERATING EXPENSE BUDGET (SECTION G).

The definitions for expense types or categories are necessary to end the practice
of accounting for expenses by system rather than by natural classification. For
instance, coffee historically may have been accounted for as food, nourishments,
office supplies, meetings and travel, and education supplies. In the future, coffee
will be expensed as "coffee" no matter how distributed or where consumed. Similarly, 2″ × 2″ gauze bandages may have been accounted for as medical supplies,
case cart expense, exchange cart expense, and others. In the future, 2″ × 2″ will
be expensed as "Gauze and Bandages" no matter how distributed and used.

If you do not see natural expense classifications in the Chart of Accounts necessary to describe, by natural expense type, all of the expenses your responsibility
will incur, call the Finance office.

V. NEW PROGRAMS AND SERVICES (DETAILED INSTRUCTIONS IN SECTION A AND WORK SHEET A)

Special attention will be given to review of new programs and services. For
budget purposes, new programs and services are defined generally as:

- functions not currently conducted but proposed for the next fiscal year to
  attain goals, objectives or plans, AND

- functions that will require additional personnel of 0.5 FTE (1,040 hours) or
  more above the staffing level proposed to accommodate current activity plus
  additional growth, OR

- functions that will have an impact of plus or minus $5,000 on nonsalary op-
  erating expenses beyond the level proposed for growth and inflation, OR

- functions that because of their nature cause the department head or responsible senior staff member to desire or require administrative review and
  approval.

Completion of the New Programs and Services Work Sheet (Form A) will require a thorough understanding of the compilation of all budget sections. Review
the instructions for all sections and keep the steps in mind as Form A is completed.
Note that establishment of a new responsibility center does not require a Form A
unless the center's activities also are new programs and services according to the
above definition.

VI. STATISTICS (DETAILED INSTRUCTIONS SECTION B AND WORK SHEET FORM B)

The statistics component is a very fundamental part of the budget and is used in almost all of the following steps. Statistics must be sufficiently descriptive of the activity of the department in order to represent the volume-related elements of revenue and expenses.

Major hospitalwide statistical forecasts are included as Appendix A-3 to these instructions. The major forecasts are not likely to change and should be used, whenever appropriate, as a basis for departmental statistical budgets.

Almost all responsibility centers are being provided with two or three forecasts of workload statistics using various assumptions and calculation methodologies.

Your budget work sheet (Form B) will allow you to use a major statistic, one of the forecast (or forecasts) of your own, whichever you feel is most descriptive of the workload for your area. After completing Form B you will refer to it for several other sections. Feel free to add your own statistics as necessary. Just follow the instructions in DETAILED INSTRUCTIONS B.

VII. CAPITAL BUDGET (DETAILED INSTRUCTIONS C AND D AND FORMS C AND D)

The capital budget is presented in two sections: (1) a Section C for the next fiscal year, and (2) a Section D for future years.

For next fiscal year's forms, detailed sheets (Forms C-1) are not initially required for items under $5,000 but may be required later. Similarly, the TEAM will not review items under $5,000. Form C does require a separation of expenditures into time blocks according to when expenditure will be required. Cash planning is extremely critical for capital requirements and your accuracy is needed as well as your reasonableness in spreading dollar requirements throughout the year rather than bunching expenditures into the early months.

Note the following general guidelines for FY 198__–8__ capital budgeting:

- Capital Assumptions are provided below.
- For renovation or construction projects that do not clearly fall under the capitalization policy, call the Finance office to discuss prior to budgeting as capital or operating expense.
- There will be no automatic carryover of current year capital items. Any current year item that will not be purchased (i.e., a purchase order will not be mailed out prior to 4-1-8__) must be rebudgeted for FY 198__–8__.

- New items for which a lease or rental agreement is envisioned as a means of financing also must be included in the capital budget if they meet the definition of capital.

The capital projection for future years (Form D) is to identify major financing needs and capital requirements in future years. You should have available your list of the capital assets in your areas as of early 198___. Refer to this list plus any other inventory documents plus your goals, objectives, and plans for the future to identify the large expenditures by year for 198___ through 198___.

VIII. REVENUE BUDGET (DETAILED INSTRUCTIONS E AND FORM E)

The revenue budget for FY 198___–8___ may be completed by one of two alternative methodologies. Alternative 1 is a fairly simple method and is adequate for smaller departments where no dynamic changes in revenue per statistic are anticipated for next year. Alternative 2 is more appropriate for larger departments with complex services. Alternative 2 must be used for any newly created Responsibility Centers where patient revenue is involved. The monthly Patient Revenue and Usage Statistics Report is an excellent source of information for the revenue budget. Please refer to this report whenever possible.

Effort should be made to compute as accurately as possible revenue per statistic as a basis for revenue projections. Consider also the potential for increased or decreased intensity and the possibility for fewer orders for services and supplies that may result from cost-containment efforts directed at physician ordering patterns by diagnosis related group (DRG).

IX. SALARY AND WAGE BUDGET (DETAILED INSTRUCTIONS F AND FORM F)

The use of 26 pay periods rather than 12 months as the budgeting format will make variance analysis and control much easier than a 12-month process.

A printout is provided by the Personnel office to show the current salary levels of staff in each Responsibility Center. Refer to this printout as necessary to complete the Salary and Wage Budget. KEEP THIS PRINTOUT SECURE AND CONFIDENTIAL.

X. OTHER OPERATING EXPENSES (DETAILED INSTRUCTIONS G AND FORMS G THROUGH G-11)

The format of the form for all other operating expenses seeks to tie expenses to statistics as accurately as possible. Note the following:

- To assure that an appropriate level of supply-related expenses in particular have been budgeted, add current year supply type accounts and annual projected totals together. Then compare to the FY 198__–8__ budgeted totals. The percentage increase should be approximately that of the inflation factor applied to supplies.
- Inflation factors are provided as Appendix 4 to these instructions.
- Zero-based work sheets are provided for natural expense types requiring this approach.

Appendix A-1
Responsibility Center Designation
Chart of Accounts Revision

I. RESPONSIBILITY CENTERS

A. Definition:

The basic accounting entity to which revenues and/or expenses can be associated with a hospital organizational unit performing specific, measurable functions.

B. Attributes:

1. The center corresponds to a box on the hospital organizational chart (or departmental organizational chart for large departments).
2. Activities are led by a specific individual who is responsible and accountable for the results and performance of activities.
3. Activities are measurable.
4. Expenses incurred are clearly definable and readily relate to the activity performed.
5. Labor assignments are consistent with supervisory lines of accountability.
6. Revenues, if generated, can be clearly matched with expenses.

C. Exceptions:

1. If activity expenses are significant (more than $100,000 per year) and are worthy of management attention, independent of organizational considerations, a separate responsibility center may be established.
2. If an income or expense category is not assignable to a specific individual for accountability, the category may be established as a separate responsibility center.

II. REVENUES

A. Definition:

The value, measured in money, recorded at the hospital's full established rates, of goods and services provided to patients or others. Revenues are to be recorded at the hospital's full established rates regardless of the amount that might ultimately be paid for the goods or services.

B. Attributes:

1. Can be associated readily with an individual patient or prescribed category or type of nonpatient.
2. Can be identified with an activity of a responsibility center.

3. Is applied consistently each time goods or services are provided.
4. Can be associated, at least generally, with the expense of providing goods or services.

C. Exceptions
   1. Repayment from nonpatients of expenses incurred to provide goods or services is not revenue and will be recorded as "Reimbursement of Costs" in the responsibility center providing the goods or services. This exception is applicable whether repayment is in full or in part.

III. EXPENSES

A. Definition:
Costs used or consumed in conducting an activity.

B. Attributes:
   1. Measurable.
   2. Identifiable with a specific responsibility center.
   3. Assignable to a responsibility center via a normal accounting system (i.e., payroll, accounts payable, inventory, etc.).
   4. Are defined by type or category as a "natural" description or definition of the nature of the expense rather than the system for accumulation or distribution of the item or service.
   5. Are defined consistently for each responsibility center by the standard deinition provided in the Chart of Accounts.

Appendix A-2
Chart of Accounts—Expenses

Natural Acct. #	Account Name & Description	General* Use	Posting* Cross-Ref.
090	Salaries and Wages Salary expense for all employees on hospital payroll	All RCs	Time Postings PR, JV
091	FICA expenses Hospital portion of Social Security taxes for all employees	All RCs	PR
092	Outside Personnel Expense for outside employment, including agency or contract. These personnel should be working in regular authorizcd positions performing duties normally assigned to regular employees	All RCs	AP
094	Salaries—S	All RCs	AP
100	Group Life Insurance Hospital portion of expense for group life insurance program	RC 960 Benefits	AP, PR
110	Employee Health Insurance Hospital portion of expense for the health insurance program	RC 960 Benefits	Empl. Part. PR AP
140	Pension Plan Expense for hospital contributions to the pension plan	RC 960 Benefits	AP
150	Disability Insurance Expense for long-term disability insurance program	RC 960 Benefits	AP
160	Workers' Compensation Insurance Hospital expense for Workers' Comp based on claim experience	RC 960 Benefits	AP
161	Workers' Compensation Small Claim Write-offs of bills not processed through Workers' Comp carrier	RC 960	AP

170	Employee Health Clinic Expense associated with employee annual physical testing and employee health clinic	RC 960 Benefits	BL
180	Unemployment Insurance Hospital expense for unemployment claims filed; rates based on experience	RC 960 Benefits	AP
185	Deferred Compensation Variable Life Hospital contribution to the deferred compensation program	RC 960 Benefits	Hosp. Part. AP Empl. Part. PR
190	Tuition Assistance Expense for hospital contribution for the tuition reimbursement program	RC 960 Benefits	AP
191	Employee Relations Expense for employee activities including picnic, etc.	RC 960 Benefits	AP
193	Employee Discount Dietary Expense for employees' 30 percent discount in the cafeteria	RC 960 Benefits	JV
200	Legal Fees Expense for general legal counsel, including retainer and other costs	RC 950	AP
202	Malpractice Insurance For Legal Fees Malpractice legal expense using malpractice insurance fund	RC 950	JV
203	Malpractice Insurance Claims Expense of actual claims paid for settlement of malpractice cases	RC 950	AP, JV
210	Audit Fees Expense associated with services performed for annual external audit	RC 907	AP
220	Credit and Collection Expense Fees paid to collection agencies for delinquent account follow-up and charge card fees	RC 901	AP, JV
230	Prof. Fees E.R. physicians	RC 779	AP
231	Prof. Fees Laboratory	RC 779	JV
232	Prof. Fees Pathology	RC 779	JV
233	Prof. Fees EKG	RC 779	JV
234	Prof. Fees EEG	RC 779	AP
236	Prof. Fees Pulmonologist	RC 779	JV

237	Prof. Fees Speech Pathology	RC 779	AP
239	Prof. Fees Urodynamics	RC 779	AP
240	Prof. Fees Anesthesiology	RC 779	AP
241	Prof. Fees Vascular Lab	RC 779	AP
	Expense for management service or interpretation of tests by physicians		
260	Gauze and Bandages	RC Patient Care	GS, JV
	Expenses for gauze, gauze bandages, and tape		
265	Processing Expense	RC 675	GS, JV
	Expense for operation of sterilization equipment		
275	Instruments	RC 675 RC 660	GS, CS, JV
	Cost of instruments used in Procedure Packs		
280	Heart Surgery Supplies	RC 660	AP, GS
	Expense for heart valves, cannulas, and related supplies used in heart cases		
285	Pump Supplies	RC 660	AP, GS
	Cost of supplies used to operate heart/lung machine for open heart cases		
286	Pacemakers	RC 660	AP, GS
	Cost of pacemaker implants		
300	Meetings and Travel	All RCs	AP
	Expense for external meetings or travel to seminars or events related to hospital, include registration fees and travel costs		
301	Board Travel	RC 950	AP
	Expense for board members' travel to attend hospital board meetings		
302	Committee Meetings	RC 962	AP, JV
	Expense for internal meetings held by hospital committees or departments		
303	Tubing	All RCs	CS, GS
	Cost of tubing used for medical gas or other equipment		
305	Needles and Syringes	All RCs	CS, GS
	Expense for needles, angiocaths, syringes, and associated equipment		

306	Gloves	All RCs	CS, GS
	Cost of gloves used in patient care departments		
308	Medical Apparel	All RC	CS, GS
	Cost of disposable medical apparel items such as shoe covers, hats, etc.		
309	Orthopedic Supplies	RC 737	CS, GS
	Expense for casting supplies, braces, and splints used in orthopedic therapy		
310	Medical/Surgical Supplies	All RC	AP, GS
	General medical supplies that have no other classification defined elsewhere in the Chart of Accounts		
311	Sutures	RC 660	CS, GS
	Cost of sutures		
312	Catheters	RC 716	GS, CS
	Expense for all types of catheters	RC 660	
		RC 721	
313	Quality Control	RC 708	AP
	Expense for quality control equipment	RC 709	
315	Nourishments	RC 619	JV
	Expenses for snacks given to patients on the Nursing Units	RC 654	
318	Radioisotopes	RC 718	AP
	Expenses for processing radioisotopes used in nuclear medicine treatment	RC 723	
320	Library Books	RC 769	AP
	Cost of purchasing books for the hospital library		
330	Drugs	RC 730	AP, JV
	Expense of drugs generally used for treatment of patients or pharmacy stock	RC 975 Patient Care	
335	Lab/Culture Expense	RC 765	JV
	Cost of lab tests performed for in-house analysis, nonpatient chargeable		
340	IV Solutions	RC 730	AP, JV
	Cost of IV solutions	RC 732	

342	Freight Expense	RC 941	AP
	Freight for all supplies and items ordered using all purchasing methods		
350	Uniforms	RC 660	AP, PR
	Expense for uniforms required for employees or patients	RC 865 RC 954	
353	Physician Education	RC 952	AP, JV
	Expense for physician education programs		
355	Minor Equipment Expense	All RC	AP, JV
	Cost of equipment purchased that meets only one of the two capitalization tests (2-year minimum life or more than $500 cost per item) and is not a supply		
360	Office Supplies	All RC	AP, GS
	Expense for general office supplies (pens, paper clips, stationery, etc.)		
365	Processor Supplies	RC 710	AP, GS
	Cost for chemicals and supplies used in X-ray film processors	RC 716 RC 721 RC 723 RC 725	
370	Medical Gases	RC 660	AP
	Expense for oxygen and other medical gases	RC 708 RC 709 RC 735 RC 736 RC 781	
380	X-Ray Film	RC 710	GS, AP
	Expense for film used for radiological testing or procedures	RC 716 RC 721 RC 723 RC 725	
385	Contrast Materials	RC 710	GS, AP
	Expense for dyes or other contrast materials used for radiological procedures	RC 716 RC 721 RC 723 RC 725	
390	Plasma and Blood	RC 702	AP
	Cost for blood and blood products		

400	Linen Expense for linen materials including sheets, blankets, etc.	RC 865	GS, AP
410	Food Cost of raw food used in Dietary or the Cafeteria	RC 803 RC 804	AP
412	Coffee Cost of coffee and supplies used for departmental coffee machines	All RC	AP
415	Dry Cleaning of Drapes Expense for drapery cleaning service	RC 850	AP
420	Napkins, Paper Goods, and Other Expense for napkins, cups, and other paper goods used in the Cafeteria and Dietary	RC 803 RC 804	GS, AP
430	China, Glass, Silver, and Utensils Expense for hardware used in the Cafeteria and Dietary	RC 803 RC 804	AP
440	Paper Supplies, General Cost of generally used paper supplies such as towels and bathroom tissue	RC 850	GS, AP
445	Cleaning Supplies Cost of general cleaning supplies such as hand soap or disinfectant cleaners	RC 803 RC 804 RC 850 RC 865	GS, AP
450	Laundry Supplies Expense for soap and other supplies used for laundry processing	RC 860	GS, AP
460	Educational Expense Expense for educational programs produced in-house or through the Education Department	All RC	AP, JV
462	Employment Expense Expense for new employee moving or travel to interview with the hospital; also for agency cost or prearranged reimbursement as conditions of employment	RC 951	AP
465	Network Expense Cost incurred using the Telenet system for educational programs	RC 952	AP

470	Miscellaneous Expense	RC 950	AP, JV
	Used for obscure expenses that can not be classified into any other account	RC 998	
471	Chaplain Expense	RC 955	AP
	Stipend for hospital Chaplain		
477	Loss/Obsolescent Inventory	RC 941	GS, JV
	Expense for loss or obsolescent write-off of supplies in storeroom		
480	Inventory Adjustments	RC 941	JV
	Expense for over or short counts for periodical physical inventories in general storeroom; will be distributed at year end to department-based or annual utilization		
490	Chapel Supplies	RC 955	AP
	Expense related to maintaining hospital chapel		
500	Equipment Maintenance	RC 660	AP
	Expense for general maintenance or repair of equipment not covered under an Engineering Department maintenance contract	RC 915	
545	Publications and Brochures	RC 953	AP
	Printing expense for hospital publications, brochures, newsletter, etc.		
547	Patient Menus	RC 803	GS, AP
	Cost for producing patient menus		
550	Medical Equipment Contract	RC 834	AP, JV
	Contract service agreement for medical equipment		
575	Community Relations	RC 953	AP
	Expense for community programs and flowers for VIPs		
580	Print Shop Cost	RC 941	GS, AP
	Cost of ink, paper, and other supplies necessary in the hospital print shop		

582	Mail Cost Expense for postage in the hospital mail room	RC 941	AP
590	Insurance, General Cost of general hospital insurance— liability, comprehensive, etc.	RC 950	AP
591	Malpractice Insurance, Other Expense Expense for miscellaneous services related to self-insurance trust, including audit, actuarial, or trustee fees	RC 950	JV, AP
610	Electricity Cost for any hospital electricity purchases	RC 832	AP
620	Natural Gas Cost for all hospital natural gas purchases	RC 832	AP
625	Fuel Oil Cost for hospital purchases of fuel oil for auxiliary generators	RC 832	AP
630	Water Cost for hospital purchases of water and sewer services	RC 832	AP
650	Electrical Air Conditioning and Refrigeration Expense for maintaining hospital cooling systems	RC 832	AP
660	Lighting Cost of general light bulbs used throughout the hospital	RC 832	GS, AP
670	Building Maintenance Expense of general building maintenance projects (moving walls, doors, etc.)	RC 832	AP
680	Painting and Decorating Expense for painting and decorating projects (paint, wallpaper, brushes, etc.)	RC 832	AP
685	Programs Expense for hospital-sponsored information programs	RC 958 RC 958	AP

686	Photography/Graphics	RC 953	AP
	Expense for photography and	RC 958	
	graphic supplies used for public		
	relations or information		
689	Dues	All RC	AP
	Cost of dues for membership in		
	professional organizations		
690	Subscriptions	All RC	AP
	Cost of subscriptions for		
	professional journals or publications		
700	Automobile Expense	RC 601	
	Expense for automobile cost	RC 832	
	reimbursement for administrators on	RC 950	
	call	RC 951	
		RC 955	
705	Parking	RC 954	AP
	Cost of approved validated parking		
	for official hospital visitors		
706	Senior Staff Parking	RC 954	AP
	Cost of senior staff parking in		
	reserved parking lot		
750	Purchased Service—Corporation	All RC	AP
	Expense for purchase of outside		
	services from corporations (no		
	supplies)		
751	Purchased Service—Individual	All RC	AP
	Expense for purchase of outside		
	service from individuals (no		
	supplies) not performing regular		
	employee duties		
752	Fellows/M.D. Training	RC 702	AP
	Cost of interns used in certain	RC 660	
	departments' training programs		
760	Telephone	RC 832	AP
	Cost of telephone equipment and		
	service		
770	Computer Rental	RC 915	AP
	Cost of computer rental	RC 941	
771	Computer Supplies	RC 915	GS, AP
	Expense for general computer	RC 941	
	supplies such as discs, ribbons, etc.		

772	Computer Software	RC 915	AP
	Expense for purchase of computer	RC 941	
	software or programming services		
775	Special Projects	RC 832	AP
780	Equipment Rental	All RC	AP
	General equipment rental costs		
781	Copy Machine Expenses	RC 702	AP
	Expense for copy machines and	RC 712	
	supplies such as dry imager, etc.	RC 736	
		RC 768	
		RC 769	
		RC 901	
		RC 920	
782	Paper Expense	All RC	GS, AP
	Expense for paper used for		
	photocopying and printing; also		
	green bar paper		
783	Forms	All RC	AP
	Expense for special forms produced		
	by outside vendors (standard		
	register, etc.)		
800	Protection Service	RC 901	AP
	Expense for protected courier		
	service to carry bank deposits to and		
	from the bank		
810	Cash Over/Short	RC 804	JV
	Expense for departments operating	RC 901	
	change funds	RC 975	
820	Television Cost	RC 950	AP
	Patient room television		
830	Employment Advertising	RC 951	AP
	Expense for recruiting advertising in	RC 601	
	newspapers and journals		
840	Microfilming	RC 768	AP
	Cost of microfilming services and	RC 901	
	supplies		
910	Reimbursement of Cost	All RC	JV
	Money received to reimburse the		
	hospital for a particular program or		
	event		

915	Property Taxes	RC 979	AP, JV
	Taxes paid on all hospital property	RC 994	
	to various governmental tax		
	authorities		
920	Rent Expense	RC 979	AP, JV
	Rent paid for hospital space used		
	away from main building, including		
	storage or office space		
921	Sales	RC 975	JV
	Sales in Apothecary		
922	Discounts on Sales	RC 975	JV
	Discounts given on Apothecary sales		
923	Sales	RC 975	J
	Sales in gift shop		
924	Sales	RC 975	J
	Parking lot fees		
925	Ground Service	RC 901	AP
	Grounds maintenance		

*RC—Responsibility Center
 GS—General Stores
 CS—Central Service

AP—Accounts Payable (Invoices)
PR—Payroll
JV—Accounting Journal Entry
BL—Patient Billing Entry

Appendix A-3
Statistical Forecast
FY 198__–8__

Name	Number	Description
Patient Days	W106	Total Hospital Patient Days
Average Daily Census	I111	Average Census
Admissions	W104	All Patients Admitted
Average Length of Stay	I110	Average Days a Patient Is Hospitalized
Percent Occupancy	I109	Monthly Hospital Occupancy Percent
Calendar Days	I102	All Days per Month
Work Days	I103	Work Days (Excluding Holidays)
Equal Distribution	I101	12 Equal Amounts

Forecast statistics can be used in spreading annual revenue or expense amounts. Each department can predict the annual amount and choose one of the above statistics for the monthly spread. The forecast values for each statistic are attached. If none of these spread factors is satisfactory, you may spread the amounts using your own basis.

STATISTICAL FORECAST
FY 198___-8___

Statistic Name & No.	Apr.	May	June	July	Aug.	Sept.	Oct.	Nov.	Dec.	Jan.	Feb.	Mar.	Total
Patient Days W106	7,324	6,991	6,598	6,597	7,240	7,187	7,173	7,151	6,434	7,523	7,076	7,689	84,983
Avg. Daily Census I111	244	226	220	213	234	240	231	238	208	243	253	248	233
Admissions W104	1,114	1,048	1,021	1,034	1,153	1,143	1,123	1,159	1,029	1,221	1,140	1,259	13,444
Avg. Length of Stay I110	6.6	6.7	6.5	6.4	6.3	6.3	6.4	6.2	6.3	6.2	6.2	6.1	6.4
% Occupancy I109	81.4	75.2	73.3	70.9	77.8	79.9	77.1	79.5	69.2	80.9	84.2	82.7	77.7
Calendar Days I102	30	31	30	31	31	30	31	30	31	31	28	31	365
Work Days I103	21	22	21	21	23	19	23	21	20	22	20	21	254

Appendix A-4
Inflation Assumptions

Type Expense	Percent Increase
Pharmaceuticals	8.0
Dietary	8.0
Utilities	13.8
Insurance	14.0
Purchased Services	8.0
Legal Fees	8.0
Audit Fees	8.0
Health Insurance	14.0
Travel Related	6.0
Office Supplies	6.0
Medical Surg Supplies, General	7.0
Fluid Administration Sets	0.0
Disposable Gloves	7.0
Disposable Apparel	0.0
Bandages/Dressings	8.0
Disposable Needles/Syringes	5.0
Foley Trays	4.0
Respiratory Therapy Products	5.0
Orthopedic Supplies	10.0
Sutures	8.5
Surgical Instruments	8.2
Surgical Sponges	0.0
Solutions	0.0
Surgical Packs	0.0
X-ray Films	2.5

Fiscal Year 198__–198__ Budget
Detailed Instructions

(Practice Forms for the following instructions appear after Section G)

ASSUMPTIONS FOR BUDGET PURPOSES

External

1. No major changes in regulatory process at state or federal level or in Joint Commission on Accreditation of Hospitals (JCAH) or fire-safety standards.
2. No changes in Prospective Payment System (PPS) after final regulations were published in the January X, 198__ Federal Register.
3. Capital costs will continue as a PPS passthrough.
4. No new competitors and no PPO or health maintenance organization (HMO) action.
5. No significant additions or defections from medical staff (i.e., comparable patient service complement).
6. No affiliations with other organizations in FY 198__ of significant budget impact.
7. No substantial change in interest rates (prime at __%).
8. Continued availability of tax-exempt debt at $2 to $2.5 million level and 75 percent of prime.
9. No labor relations activity.
10. Relative stability in the local area job market for most classes.
11. Continued reliance on surveys of wage rates as adequate indicators of need to adjust rates.
12. Inflation impact at rates shown in inflation factor section of budget instructions.

Internal

1. Trends in utilization will be consistent with current year and forecasting of service statistics at the department level will be adequate for the initial modeling of PPS impact.
2. If modeling of budgeted utilization and costs reveals substantial losses of

Medicare net revenue, the adjustments will be targeted for both utilization and costs prior to recommending a budget package.

3. Financial reports at 12/31 and 1/31 will be adequate as a baseline to project next FY trends (i.e., no substantial misstatements).
4. No prior year Medicare adjustments will affect bottom line.
5. Rate increases will not be required 4/1 as result of continued strong cash and bottom-line position. Uncertainty now is capital requirements.
6. Salary and wage increases will not be required on an across-the-board basis on 4/1 and surveys will determine when.
7. Improvements in benefits package will be recommended.
8. Consulting expenses will be up because of studies for cancer center, information system, burn program, space plan, and Doctors Building acquisition (unless capitalized).
9. Earnings from Hospital Foundation and X Fund will be included appropriately in budget.
10. No major (although some minor) service changes are expected.
11. Continued emphasis will be placed on charity, with Hill-Burton included at estimated requirement level.
12. Bad debts will be projected at current levels.
13. Levels of insurance coverage for patients will be estimated at current experience.
14. No increase in Medicaid utilization will be projected.
15. No use of funded depreciation will be projected. Funded depreciation will be a contingency for the Doctors Building acquisition.
16. Doctors Building acquisition will be treated as a stand-alone decision apart from budget, including feasibility, financing, and organizational changes.
17. Capitalization policy will remain at $500 per item and two-year minimum life.
18. No current-year capital will be carried over automatically.

A. NEW PROGRAMS AND SERVICES

1. Put Responsibility Center name and number in spaces provided in the upper left corner.
2. Place program or service name on line 1.
3. Place description in space provided on front side of form.

   USE A SEPARATE FORM FOR EACH NEW PROGRAM
   AND SERVICE

   Be sure to include names of participating physicians, sources of patients, description of services, levels of charges, equipment used, need for new personnel, and impact on operating expenses if appropriate for revenue-producing services; OR, be sure to include description of expense reduction, resources substituted, equipment used, need for personnel, if appropriate.
4. On the reverse side of the form use the blanks provided to calculate the various types of budget impact this program or service will have. If there will be a reduction in any of the elements listed, place brackets [ ] around the item reduced or decreased.

   New programs and services will be reviewed before remaining components of the budget. If the program is *not approved,* these numbers will be used to adjust the other components of the budget to eliminate the impact.

   BE SURE TO INCLUDE THESE ELEMENTS IN CALCULATIONS
   FOR REMAINING PARTS OF THE BUDGET.

5. Number the pages in the upper right corner and show the number of pages involved, i.e., Page 1 of 4, Page 2 of 4, etc.
6. Department head must initial in "Submitted By."
7. Senior staff must initial in "Reviewed By" after assuring that forms are complete and the new programs and services are consistent with department's and hospital's goals and objectives and long-range plans.

B. STATISTICAL FORECAST

1. Put Responsibility Center name and number in spaces provided in the upper left corner.
2. Place statistic name and number, if known, on left side of form. You may want to forecast only one statistic for your RC or you may need more than one. For example:
   Inpatient Tests and Outpatient Tests
   Total Procedures
   Patient Days W106
   Emergency Room Visits
3. Whatever forecast you use, you must choose at least *one* statistic. Please enter the monthly amounts and total of the statistic forecast most representative of your plans for next year.
4. If a statistical forecast is required for an RC and none is turned in, we will use patient days as the default.
5. Department heads must initial in "Submitted By."
6. Senior staff must initial in "Reviewed By" after assuring that the forecast is complete and consistent with the department's and hospital's goals and objectives.
7. Keep in mind that this statistic forecast will be used in several other parts of the budget:
   - Revenue Projection
   - Expense Projection
   - Month-to-Month Spreading (spread factor)

C. CAPITAL BUDGET

1. Use separate forms for clinical and nonclinical equipment. Check the appropriate box in upper right corner to indicate clinical or nonclinical.
2. Enter Responsibility Center name and number in blanks provided in upper left corner.
3. For each item or project to be submitted enter the following:
   a. Expend. Class (Expenditure Class): Enter one of the following to describe the primary reason for submitting the item or project:
      (1). Accreditation/Licensure/Code Compliance: Item or project is necessary to maintain status.
      (2). Replacement: Item or project will replace existing equipment or facilities. In the description area for replacement items, describe the item or facility to be replaced.
      (3). Growth: Item or project is necessary to provide capacity to handle the projected increase in volume of services budgeted in revenue and expense budget for FY 198__.
      (4). Revenue Substitution: Item or project will reduce expense of some nature in the next and future budget periods.
      (5). New Program: Item or project will provide for a completely new service not currently offered. If the revenue or expense impact of the new program or service is greater than 3 percent of the current year's revenue *or* expense budget (actual and projected for FY 198__–198__) then a New Program and Service Form also must be submitted (see Section A, above).
   b. Rev.? Y or N: Enter Y for Yes and N for No if the item or project is revenue producing.
   c. Qty. (Quantity): Enter the quantity or number of items requested.
   d. Vendor: Enter the most likely vendor for the item or project. If no vendor has been selected, put "unknown" or if there are only two or three vendors likely, list them. If Engineering Department will provide, put Eng.
   e. Item or Project Description: describe briefly the project's name or nature. Be sure to list installation and construction separately (see example). If the item or project is a replacement, describe the item or facility being replaced.
   f. Mo. of Order (Month of Order): Enter the month and year, i.e., 2/8__ or 11/8__, in which the order for the item or project will be placed by the Purchasing Department. Be sure to allow sufficient time for reviews, approvals (including certificate of need [CON] if required) and processing time.
   g. Total Cost by Pay. or Proj. Comp. Date (Total Cost by Payment or Project Completion Date): In the column noting the time frames 4/8__–9/8__,

10/8___–3/8___, and After 3/8___, enter the total cost of the time or project ACCORDING TO THE TIME THE PAYMENT TO THE VENDOR WILL BE MADE OR THE PROJECT WILL BE FINISHED. Be sure to allow for down payments, payments at delivery, installation time, and acceptance time. More than one payment period might be entered per item (see example) or if installation or renovation is involved and listed separately, each part may have more than one payment period.

If the item or project total cost is more than $5,000, a Detailed Capital Expenditure Form (Form C-1) must be completed for each item and attached to the Capital Budget sheet for FY 198___–8___.

h. Cost Source: Enter one of the following to describe the source of the cost listed:

M—From Engineering

V—From vendor or salesman direct

P—From Purchasing Department

C—From vendor catalog

E—Your estimate

i. Maint. Agree. (Maintenance Agreement): If maintenance is charged separately for in the first year of our ownership, i.e., the warranty does not provide for maintenance, parts, and repairs, enter the amount of the maintenance agreement for the remaining portion of FY 198___–8___.

4. Number pages and show number of pages involved, i.e., Page 1 of 4, Page 2 of 4, etc., for clinical and nonclinical forms separately.

5. Total each of the three columns with dollar amounts entered for "Total Cost by Pay or Proj. Comp. Date" and ENTER TOTALS ON LAST PAGE ONLY. Do not subtotal each page.

6. Department Head must initial in "Submitted By."

7. Senior staff must initial in "Reviewed By" after assuring that forms are complete and items or projects submitted are consistent with goals and objectives of responsibility center and hospital. For items under $5,000, senior staff initials indicate support and approval for acquisition if capital budget allocation permits. Approval on this form will *not* replace the need for a Purchase Requisition, which must be submitted at the appropriate time to initiate an order.

C. CAPITAL BUDGET (Example)

FY 198__8__

Responsibility Center:
Name ___Nursing___
Number ___987___

Clinical: ___✓___
NonClinical: _____
Page 1 of 1

Expend. Class	Rev.? Y or N	Qty.	Vendor	Item or Project Description	Mo. of order	Total Cost by Pay. or Proj. Comp. Date			Cost Source	Maint. Agree.
						4/8 —9/8	10/8 —3/8	Aft. 3/8		
C	Y	1	Picker	Oncology Center	4/8	$100,000	$1,250,000	$50,000	V	-0-
C	N	1	SJB	Renovation for Center	5/8		80,000		M	-0-
C	N	1	Steelcase	Model 1480 Desk w/type standard	1/8		800		P	-0-
B	N	4	Ericson	Microfiche camera reader-printer unit (replaces Kodak Model 850)	2/8		5,000	15,000	E	500
					Totals	100,000	1,335,800	65,000		

Submitted By: ___E.F.___ Reviewed By: ___L.B.___

D. CAPITAL PROJECTIONS

1. This projection for future years requires no separation of clinical and non-clinical equipment.
2. Enter Responsibility Center name and number in blanks provided in upper left corner.
3. For each item or project to be submitted enter the following:
   a. Expend. Class (Expenditure Class): Enter one of the following to describe the primary reason for submitting the item or project:
      (1). Accreditation/Lincensure/Code Compliance: Item or project is necessary to maintain status.
      (2). Replacement: Item or project will replace existing equipment or facilities. In the description area for replacement items, describe the item or facility to be replaced.
      (3). Growth: Item or project is necessary to provide capacity to handle the projected increase in volume of services budgeted in revenue and expense budget for FY 198___.
      (4). Revenue Substitution: Item or project will reduce expense of some nature in the next and future budget periods.
      (5). New Program
   b. Rev.? Y or N: Enter Y for Yes and N for No if the item or project is revenue producing.
   c. Qty. (Quantity): Enter the quantity or number of items requested.
   d. Vendor: Enter the most likely vendor for the item or project. If no vendor has been selected, enter "unknown," or if there are only two or three vendors likely, list them. If Maintenance Department will provide, put_____.
   e. Item or Project Description: Describe briefly by name the item or nature of the project. Be sure to list installation and construction separately (see example). If the item or project is a replacement, describe the item or facility being replaced.

      It may be useful to refer to the printout included in your package when considering replacements. This printout may not list all items in your area accurately but may provide some assistance.
   f. Cost by Year or Pay. or Proj. Comp. (Cost by Year of Payment or Project Completion): Enter the projected total payment to be made for each item in each year that payment will be made. Precision is not as important in this form as in the FY 198___–8___ form for capital budget; however, general timing of cash demand should be presented. Estimates or even guesses of future year costs are required. Please make every attempt to include a reasonable amount for each item.

    g. Cost Source: Enter one of the following to describe the source of the cost listed:

    M—From Engineering

    V—From vendor or salesman direct

    P—From Purchasing Department

    C—From vendor catalog

    E—Your estimate

4. Number pages and show number of pages involved, i.e., Page 1 of 4, Page 2 of 4, etc.
5. Total each of the four columns with dollar amounts entered for "Total Cost by Pay. or Proj. Comp. Date" and ENTER TOTALS ON LAST PAGE ONLY. Do not subtotal each page.
6. Department Head must initial in "Submitted By."
7. Senior staff must initial in "Reviewed By" after assuring that forms are complete and items or projects submitted are consistent with departmental and hospital long-range plan.

D. CAPITAL BUDGET PROJECTIONS (Example)

FY 198___ -8___

Page 1___ of ___1___

Responsibility Center:
Name ___Nursing___
Number ___987___

Expend. Class	Rev.? Y or N	Qty.	Vendor	Item or Project Description	Cost by Year of Pay. or Proj. Comp.				Cost Source
					FY 198___	FY 198___	FY 198___	FY 198___	
B	N	1	IBM	Selectric Typewriter (replaces Underwood manual)			$1,000		V
E	N	1	Steelcase	Office Modular Furniture System		$15,000	15,000	$20,000	E
				Totals	—	15,000	16,000	20,000	

Submitted By: ___E.F.___

Admin. Review: ___L.B.___

E. REVENUE BUDGET: ALTERNATIVE 1

1. Enter Responsibility Center name and number in the upper left corner.
2. Lines 1 through 6 are self-explanatory.
3. Line 7 requires an analysis (objective or subjective) to determine whether an increase in revenue intensity of services per production unit will occur over the next 16 months (December 198__ through March 198__ plus 12 months of FY 198__–8__). In departments where production units are composed of a broad range of prices for services, an increase in utilization or ordering patterns of higher priced services will alter the current revenue per production unit position. Each department should examine the detailed makeup of services to determine whether a rationale exists for inflating the revenue per production unit.

   DO NOT APPLY ANY CHARGE INCREASE ASSUMPTION IN THIS ANALYSIS. USE CURRENT CHARGES ONLY.

   If rationale exists for assuming an intensity increase in revenue per production unit, if possible calculate rather than estimate this percentage. Help is available in the Finance Office to make these calculations. When the percentage is determined, record the percentage in decimal form plus 1.0 in the spare line 7. This will be used in later steps.
4. Line 8 provides for the opposite effect discussed in paragraph 3 above. If diminished revenue per production unit is anticipated, subtract the percentage in decimal form from 1.0 and enter the result in the space provided in step 8.
5. Line 9 is self-explanatory.
6. Line 10 requires the calculation of total revenue by multiplying the adjusted rate per unit by the budgeted production units for FY 198__–8__ from Section B. There are several options for this step:
   a. Record units in the blanks provided for inpatient (IP) and outpatient (OP) statistics and perform the arithmetic to complete the step.
   b. Record only total IP and OP units rather than the monthly breakdown and multiply by the adjusted revenue per units (e) or (f) in total only. If only total units are used, a spread factor must be entered in line 12.
   c. Do nothing and the Finance Office will perform the arithmetic using the production units in Section B and data you compute through line 9.
7. Line 11 requires the simple adding of IP and OP total revenue (g & h).
8. Line 12 requires specification of the spread factor used (or to be used if the Finance Office completes calculations) for the month-to-month distribution of revenue.

E. REVENUE BUDGET: ALTERNATIVE 2

1. Enter Responsibility Center name and number in the upper left corner.
2. Check whether the page is for inpatient or outpatient revenue in the upper right corner.
3. For each revenue service or category of revenue services, list the following:
   a. Serv. Name (Service Name): List name of revenue service or category description.
   b. Code No. (Code Number): List input number if for an individual service or item.
   c. Charge or Rate: Enter the current charge for individual services or items OR the average current rate per unit in a category of services.
   d. Multi. Factor (Multiplying Factor): This represents the number of times this service or item is to be applied for a major statistical category. For example, if a test is done on the average twice per admission, then the Multi. Factor would be 2.0 and the statistic would be admissions.
   e. Statistic: List the statistic name or number appropriate to be used to determine revenue by month (see Section B).
   f. For each month multiply the charge or rate by the monthly statistic appropriate for the service times the Multi. Factor (c × d × e) and enter the result month by month.

   OR

   Multiply the charge or rate by the annual total statistic for the service times the Multi. Factor and enter the result in the Total column. The Finance Office will spread the annual Total monthly using the monthly distributed statistic.

   OR

   Do nothing and the Finance Office will finish.
   g. If a month-by-month computation is made, total 12 months horizontally and enter the sum Total.
4. Repeat the sequences in paragraph 3 until all revenue service categories are provided.
5. Complete the above steps for both inpatient and outpatient services.
6. Number the pages and show the number of pages involved (i.e., Page 1 of 4, Page 2 of 4, etc.) for Inpatient and Outpatient revenue SEPARATELY (i.e., two sets).
7. If either a month-by-month or annual computation was made, total all computed columns vertically and enter the total on the last page of the Inpatient or Outpatient set. Do not subtotal each page.

F. SALARY, WAGE, AND FICA BUDGET

Forms F through F-3

1. Enter Responsibility Center name and number on Forms F through F-3 in the space provided in the upper right corner.
2. Beginning with Form F, complete the computations necessary to convert the monthly volumes of the statistic most descriptive of the application of personnel for the responsibility center into 26 biweekly amounts. Most statistics will have some relationship to patient days; therefore, the conversion factors in Form F, Column 1, are based on an anticipated distribution of patient days biweekly.

   If a patient-day-related statistic does not describe the application of personnel in your responsibility center (i.e., an administrative fixed staff center or a small department), do not complete Form F.
3. Transcribe the Adjusted Stat. Value from Form F to Form F-3, column 2, by pay period;

   OR

   If no computation was made, enter 14 (for days per pay period) if you wish to compute productive hours on a daily basis for each pay period;

   OR

   Enter 1 for each pay period if you wish to compute production hours on a pay-period basis.
4. Use Form F-1 to compute the average regular pay rate for employees in the responsibility center. Note: If you wish to develop an alternative to Form F-1 for this purpose, you may do so. Be prepared to discuss the use of alternatives with _____ at the time your budget is completed.

   Form F-1 may be completed as follows (see example Form F-1):

   a. Enter the name or the title of each employee in the Responsibility Center. Larger departments may find it easier to enter one line for employees in each job type. Refer to the salary detail printout provided in your folder. If new employees are proposed for growth, use the caption "New (Title)-Growth" instead of name. If new employees are proposed for new programs and services, use the caption "New (Title)-P & S" instead of name. If authorized positions are currently unfilled, use the caption "Vacant."

   b. Under "FTE" enter the full-time equivalent value for each employee or job type currently authorized or proposed. If you do not know how to compute the FTE value, call _____ for help.

    c. Under Current Hr. Rate (Current Hourly Rate) enter the REGULAR HOURLY RATE from the salary detail you maintain for your staff. For proposed or vacant positions, you must assume a rate that will be paid. *Do not include any premium, call, or differential pay in this amount.*

    d. If the employee will receive a merit increase after the day of the salary detail printout (12-20-8__) but before April 1, 198__, enter the amount of the increase (not percentage) in the column titled "Merit FY 198____."

    e. Add the Current Hourly Rate to the Merit FY 198__ hourly amount and enter the sum in the column titled "Hr. Rate 4-1-198__."

    f. Multiply the FTE value by the Hr. Rate 4-1-198__ value by 2,080 and enter the result under "Annual Amount." This step is necessary to achieve a proper weighing for part-time employees in the final calculation of average hourly rate.

    g. For the month anticipated for the employee's merit increase in FY 198__-8__ and each subsequent month, enter the merit amount per month anticipated.

    h. If more than one Form F-1 is used, number the forms completed and show the number of forms (Page 1 of 2, etc.) Enter totals on last page only. Do not subtotal each page.

    i. Follow the remaining steps:

        (1) Multiply total FTEs by 2,080 and divide the result by 12.

        (2) Add $1/12$ of the Annual Amount total to each month's Merit Amount total.

        (3) Divide the sum by the result of (1) above.

    j. Enter the result by month on Form F-3 for each pay period ending in that month under the Form F-3 column titled "Reg. Pay Rate" (column 8).

5. Use Form F-2 to calculate shift differential and call pay on a biweekly basis and to adjust that amount per pay periods with holidays. Official holidays for FY 198__-8__, with pay period ending (PPE) date, will be:

Memorial Day	May 28, 198__	PPE 6-9-8__
July 4th	July 4, 198__	PPE 7-7-8__
Labor Day	September 3, 198__	PPE 9-15-8__
Thanksgiving	November 22, 198__	PPE 11-24-8__
Christmas	December 25, 198__	PPE 1-5-8__
New Year's	January 1, 198__	PPE 1-5-8__

Enter the biweekly regular or holiday week amounts for each pay period under the columns on Form F-3 titled "Shift Diff. Amt." (column 10) and "Call Pay Amt." (column 11).

6. Now complete Form F-3:

a. Enter the Productive Hours per Statistic in column 3 based on either personnel hours per value in column 2 (from step 3 and Form F) or hours per day or pay period.

b. Multiply columns 2 and 3 for each pay period and enter the result in column 4.

c. Determine an appropriate percentage factor for nonproductive hours as they relate to productive hours in your department. Be sure to allow for greater nonproductive time during low-volume or holiday pay periods. Enter the percentage value decimal equivalent by pay period in column 5. Multiply columns 4 and 5 and enter the result in column 6.

OR

Do not determine a nonproductive factor and enter hours anticipated from schedules, etc., in column 6.

d. Add the productive and nonproductive hours from columns 4 and 6 and enter the sum in column 7.

e. Multiply columns 7 and 8 and enter the result in column 9.

f. Determine the amount involved in any future levels programs if your department is approved for such a program and enter the additional dollars in column 12.

g. Determine a suitable biweekly amount for overtime and enter in column 13. NOTE: Overtime logically should not be budgeted in every pay period but should apply to periods of peak volume or nonproductive time or during special projects.

h. Add the amounts biweekly for columns 9, 10, 11, 12, and 13 and enter the result in column 14.

i. The Finance Office will compute the remaining portions to determine monthly budget amounts and the FICA budget.

G. OPERATING EXPENSE BUDGET SUMMARY

(NonSalary)

1. Put Responsibility Center name and number in the upper left corner.
2. Use the Chart of Accounts to select expense types (natural accounts) that pertain to your area. Expense types may have different meanings for FY 198__–198__ than for prior years. Be sure to read the definition and list all expense types appropriate for expenses that will be incurred next year. Note that natural expenses are descriptive of the expense itself, not of the distribution system or any other factor (i.e., bandages in Gauze and Bandages (#260) versus the old Case Cart Expense that might have included bandages in the past).

   Enter the expense numbers and names in the spaces provided (exclude Salaries and FICA).
3. If the expense type is listed below, the expense must be zero-base determined. Zero base involves an itemization of elements of the expense rather than a projection based on historical trends or factors. Special forms have been provided for expenses listed below with an asterisk (*). Other expenses listed below are unique to the Responsibility Center shown, and general form (G-11) is provided in the blank form set for compilation.

   *092 Outside Personnel
    191 Employee Relations (RC 960)
   *300 Meetings and Travel
    301 Board Travel (RC 960)
   *302 Committee Meetings
   *355 Minor Equipment
   *460 Educational Expense
    545 Publications and Brochures (RC 953)
    685 Programs (RC 958)
   *689 Dues
   *690 Subscriptions
   *750 Purchased Service—Corporation
   *751 Purchased Service—Individual
    775 Special Projects (RC 832)
   *780 Equipment Rental

   If you feel it is necessary to apply any expense above not noted by an asterisk (*) in your department, call _____or _____ before using the expense.
4. For any zero-based expense category, complete the special form provided. If no special form is provided, list description of events, projects, or trans-

actions that will comprise the expense, the amounts, and the month expenses will be incurred on a General Zero-Based Expense Compilation Work Sheet (Form G-11). BE SURE TO USE INFLATED AMOUNTS.
5. Total the expenses for each Zero-Base Form by month.
6. Transfer the month-by-month amount and the total for the year to the Operating Expense Budget (Form G) on the line you set up for expense.
7. Finish the zero-based expense lines by dashes (–) in the columns on the Operating Expense Budget (Form G) in the columns titled "rate," "Inflation Factor," "Multi. Factor." and "Stat."
8. For all other lines perform the following steps for each expense type:
   a. Determine the rate or expense amount expected per workload statistics or increments of workload statistics involved with the expense (i.e., Office Supplies of $10 per patient day). Enter the rate in the "Rate" column.
   b. Determine the appropriate inflation factor for the expense type (see General Instructions). Convert the inflation percentage to decimal equivalent and add to 1.0 (i.e., 6% = 1.06).
   c. If applicable, enter the Multi. Factor (multiplication factor) needed to convert the rate basis to the statistical basis most appropriate to spread the expense month to month.
   For example: If Office Supply items cost $10 and are used for 50 percent of all admissions, the following would be entered.

Rate	*Inflat. Factor*	*Multi. Factor*	*Stat.*
$10	1.06	0.5	Admissions

   If a multiple of the rate per statistic is not applicable, enter 1.0.
   d. Identify the statistic (Stat.) that best describes the distribution of the expense type month to month (see Section B).
   e. For each month, multiply the Rate by the Inflation Factor times the Multi. Factor times the monthly Statistic (A × B × C × D) and enter the amount in each monthly column. Total the columns horizontally and enter the annual amount under "Total,"
   OR
   Multiply the Rate times the Inflation Factor times the Multi. Factor times the annual total for the Statistic (A × B × C × D) and enter the amount in the "Total" column. The Finance Office will spread the month-to-month amounts using the Statistic specified.
   OR
   Do nothing and the Finance Office will finish.
9. Repeat for all other nonzero-based expense lines.
10. If the computation process described in paragraphs 8 and 9 is not appropriate for the expense type, compile monthly amounts using the appropri-

ate methodology and enter the month-to-month amounts and annual total.

11. Number each page and show the total number of pages (i.e., Page 1 of 2, Page 2 of 2) in the upper right corner.

12. If all compilations have been entered horizontally for all expense lines, total the columns vertically and enter the totals on the last page of the set. Do not subtotal each page.

Practice Forms

A. NEW PROGRAMS AND SERVICES
Responsibility Center
Name:_____

Number:_____

1. New Program or Service Name:_____
2. Describe the new program or service briefly:

(Continued)

A. NEW PROGRAMS (continued)

3. Include in the budget detail all the relevant budget data. Identify below each of the budget elements added into your budget for this new program or service. If program is to reduce expenses, place brackets around expenses.

   a. Month/year of start-up: _____

   b. Workload statistics added: _____

   c. How spread (ask finance office for spread factor this year): _____

   d. Revenue/charge per statistic $_____

   e. Total revenue (b × d): $_____

   f. Personnel hours per statistic: _____

   g. Total personnel hours added (deleted) (b × f): _____

   h. Full-time equivalents added (deleted) (g ÷ 2,080): _____

   i. Pay rate per hour: $_____

   j. Total labor included (excluded) salary and wage budget (g × i): $_____

   k. Other expenses added (decreased):

Natural Acct. #	Name	Amount
_____	_____	$_____
_____	_____	_____
_____	_____	_____
_____	_____	_____
_____	_____	_____
_____	_____	_____

   l. Total other expenses added (decreased): $_____

   m. Net gross income (e minus j minus k): $_____

   n. Capital Budget FY 198__–8__ Total Cost: $_____

Submitted By:_____   Reviewed By:_____

B. STATISTICAL BUDGET

FY 198___8___

Responsibility Center:

Name: _____

Number: _____

Statistic Name & No.	Apr.	May	June	July	Aug.	Sept.	Oct.	Nov.	Dec.	Jan.	Feb.	Mar.	Total

Submitted By: _____ Reviewed By: _____

B. STATISTICAL FORECAST–1

Responsibility Center:
Name:____ICU____
Number:____650____

FY 198____–8

Statistic Name & No.	Apr.	May	June	July	Aug.	Sept.	Oct.	Nov.	Dec.	Jan.	Feb.	Mar.	Total
ICU Days W191	271	258	244	243	268	266	265	264	238	278	262	284	3,141

B. STATISTICAL FORECAST-2

Responsibility Center:
Name: 7th Floor
Number: 637

FY 198___-8___

Statistic Name & No.	Apr.	May	June	July	Aug.	Sept.	Oct.	Nov.	Dec.	Jan.	Feb.	Mar.	Total
7th Floor Days W171	1,218	1,163	1,099	1,095	1,204	1,197	1,193	1,189	1,070	1,251	1,177	1,279	14,135

B. STATISTICAL FORECAST–3

Responsibility Center:

Name: CSU

Number: 654

FY 198__–8

Statistic Name & No.	Apr.	May	June	July	Aug.	Sept.	Oct.	Nov.	Dec.	Jan.	Feb.	Mar.	Total
CSU Days W211	209	200	188	189	207	205	206	204	184	215	202	220	2,429

B. STATISTICAL FORECAST–4

Responsibility Center:
Name: 6th Floor
Number: 635

FY 198__–8__

Statistic Name & No.	Apr.	May	June	July	Aug.	Sept.	Oct.	Nov.	Dec.	Jan.	Feb.	Mar.	Total
6th Floor Days W161	1,259	1,202	1,134	1,132	1,244	1,235	1,232	1,228	1,105	1,292	1,216	1,321	14,600

C. CAPITAL BUDGET

Responsibility Center:

Name: _____

Number: _____

FY 198___-8___

Expend. Class	Rev.? Y or N	Qty.	Vendor	Item or Project Description	Mo. of Order	Total Cost by Pay. or Proj. Comp. Date			Cost Source	Maint. Agree.
						4/8 – 9/8	10/8 – 3/8	Aft 3/8		
Totals										

Submitted By: _____   Reviewed By: _____

Form C-1. Detailed Capital Expenditure Form
FY 198___ Capital Plan

1. Department	Cost Center	Revenue Center

2. Item Requested and Quantity

3. Manufacturer	4. Model Number

5. Additional Information

6. Total Estimated Cost	(A) Base Price_____
	(B) Freight_____
	(C) Installation_____
	(D) Other_____

Asset Life: Years:

7. Justification (Reason for Expenditure)

8. Expenditure Classification	Revenue Generating	Non-revenue Generating	9. Estimated Annual Profit (see PRO FORMA)
(A) Accreditation/Licensure/ Code Compliance			(A) Estimated Annual Total Add to Operating Income $
(B) Replacement			(B) Est. Annual Operating Cost, Including Maint. or Serv. Agreement $_____
(C) Growth			
(D) Resource Substitution			
(E) New Program			

10. Approvals

(A) Department Head	(D) Administrator
(B) Assistant Administrator	(E) Executive Committee
(C) Vice President for Finance	(F) Board

Pro Forma Operating Income Statement
198__ Capital Plan

Computation of Annual Contribution to Operating Income

	Total	
A. Section I		
Gross Operating Revenue:	$	%
Inpatient	_____	
Outpatient	_____	
Other Income	_____	
Total	_____	100%
Revenue Deductions		
Contractual Adjustment	_____	
Bad Debt Provision	_____	
Total	_____	
Net Operating Revenue	_____	
B. Section II		
Operating Expenses:		
Payroll—Administration & General	_____	
Payroll—Nursing & Ancillary	_____	
Payroll—Support Services	_____	
Total Payroll	_____	_____
Operating Cost	_____	_____
Depreciation	_____	_____
Rental—Real Estate & Equipment	_____	_____
Interest	_____	_____
Amortization	_____	_____
Total Operating Expenses	_____	_____
Net Operating Income	_____	_____

	Assumed Cost-Based Reimb. %	Assumed Charge-Based Reimb. %	Total
Inpatient	_____%	_____%	
Outpatient	_____%	_____%	_____%
	_____%	_____%	_____%

CAPITAL BUDGET PLAN
Problem and Solution Statement

Project Title_____ **Accountable Manager**_____

Problem Statement
1. Describe the problem:

2. Identify medical and hospital staff members who have helped define the problem:

(Continued)

(Problem and Solution Statement) continued
Solution Statement
1. Describe briefly the proposed solution to the problem:

2. Discuss how the proposed project will resolve the problem:

3. Identify available alternative solutions, and why they were rejected:

4. Describe the standard uses associated with the project:

_____   _____
Signature (of person completing form)   Date

D. CAPITAL PROJECTIONS

Responsibility Center:

FY 198___ Through 198___

Name: _____

Number: _____

Expend. Class	Rev.? Y or N	Qty.	Vendor	Item or Project Description	Cost by Year of Pay. or Proj. Comp.				Cost Source
					FY 1986	FY 1987	FY 1988	FY 1989	
			Totals						

Submitted By: _____

Admin. Review: _____

E. REVENUE BUDGET: ALTERNATIVE 1, CALCULATIONS
FY 198__–8__

Responsibility Center:

Name:_____

Number:_____

1. Enter FY 198__ year-to-date (YTD) inpatient revenue $_____
   from revenue and expense report for November 198__

2. Enter FY 198__ YTD inpatient production units from $_____
   statistics history.

3. Divide line 1 by line 2 and enter result for current year $_____ (a)
   revenue at current prices per production unit.

4. Enter FY 198__ YTD outpatient revenue from revenue $_____
   and expense report for November, 198__.

5. Enter FY 198__ outpatient production units from sta- $_____
   tistics forecast (see above).

6. Divide line 4 by line 5 and enter result for current $_____ (b)
   prices per production unit.

7. Intensity increase? $_____ (c)
   No: Go to step *10*
   Yes: Enter decimal equivalent of percentage increase
        expected plus 1 (i.e., 4% = 1.04)

8. Diminished revenue? $_____ (d)
   No: Go to step *10*
   Yes: Subtract decimal equivalent of percentage de-
        crease expected from 1 (i.e., 4% = .96)

9. Multiply to find adjusted revenue per unit
   Inpatient   (a) $_____ × (c) or (d) _____ = $_____ (e)
   Outpatient (b) $_____ × (c) or (d) _____ = $_____ (f)

10. Compute revenue per month or year by multiplying revenue per unit
    (a) and (b) OR (e) and (f), if adjusted by budgeted statistic for
    FY 198__–8__ production units.
    If you desire, the Finance Office will make these computations for you.

Inpatient (IP)			Outpatient (OP)	
April	_____ =	$_____	_____	_____
May	_____ =	_____	_____	_____
June	_____ =	_____	_____	_____
July	_____ =	_____	_____	_____
Aug.	_____ =	_____	_____	_____
Sept.	_____ =	_____	_____	_____
Oct.	_____ =	_____	_____	_____
Nov.	_____ =	_____	_____	_____
Dec.	_____ =	_____	_____	_____
Jan.	_____ =	_____	_____	_____
Feb.	_____ =	_____	_____	_____
Mar.	_____ =	_____	_____	_____
Total	_____ =	_____ (g)	_____	_____ (h)

11. Sum (g) + (h) = $_____ (Total Revenue)

12. Spread factor if Total IP or OP only was computed (use spread factor from statistics forecast above):_____

E. REVENUE BUDGET: ALTERNATIVE 2

Responsibility Center:

Name: _____

Number: _____

Inpatient: _____

Outpatient: _____

Page _____ of _____

198___–198___ Revenue

Serv. Name	Code No.	Charge or Rate	Multi. Factor	Statistic	Apr.	May	June	July	Aug.	Sept.	Oct.	Nov.	Dec.	Jan.	Feb.	Mar.	Total
Totals																	

F. SALARY AND WAGE BUDGET: STATISTICAL CONVERSION
Responsibility Center:

Name:_____

Number:_____

Pay Period Ending Date	1 Conversion Factor	2 Monthly Statistical Value		3 Adjusted Statistical Value
4-14	.04022			
4-28	.04002	_____	=	_____
5-12	.03759			
5-26	.03815	_____	=	_____
6-9	.03556			
6-23	.03723	_____	=	_____
7-7	.03465			
7-21	.03506	_____	=	_____
8-4	.03600			
8-18	.03840	_____	=	_____
9-1	.03950			
9-15	.03840			
9-29	.03947	_____	=	_____
10-13	.03821			
10-27	.03812	_____	=	_____
11-10	.03994			
11-24	.03827	_____	=	_____
12-8	.03637			
12-22	.03519	_____	=	_____
1-5	.03426			
1-19	.04098	_____	=	_____
2-2	.04001			
2-16	.04143	_____	=	_____
3-2	.04159			
3-16	.04260			
3-30	.04278	_____	=	_____

F-1. SALARY AND WAGE BUDGET: AVERAGE HOURLY RATE COMPUTATION

Responsibility Center:
Name: _____
Number: _____

Page _____ of _____

Employee Name/Title	FTE	Current Hr. Rate	Merit FY 198__	Hr. Rate 4-1-198__	Annual Amount	Merit Month and Amount											
						Apr.	May	June	July	Aug.	Sept.	Oct.	Nov.	Dec.	Jan.	Feb.	Mar.

F-2. SALARY AND WAGE BUDGET: SHIFT DIFFERENTIAL AND CALL PAY COMPUTATION, BIWEEKLY

Responsibility Center:

Name:_____

Number:_____

Regular Pay Period: Shift Differential

Rate/Hr.		Hours at Diff.	Total
$2.00	×	_____	$_____
1.25	×	_____	_____
0.80	×	_____	_____
0.50	×	_____	_____
		Regular Total	_____

Holiday Pay Period Additions

Rate/Hr.		Hours at Diff.	Total
$2.00	×	_____	$_____
1.25	×	_____	_____
0.80	×	_____	_____
0.50	×	_____	_____
		Holiday Additions	_____
		Holiday Total	_____

Call Pay Regular Pay Period

Rate/Hr.		Hours on Call	Total
$_____	×	_____	$_____
_____	×	_____	_____
		Regular Total	_____

Holiday Pay Additions

Rate/Hr.		Hours on Call	Total
$_____	×	_____	$_____
_____	×	_____	_____
		Holiday Additions	_____
		Holiday Totals	_____

F-3. WAGE, SALARY AND FICA BUDGET

Responsibility Center: _____

Name: _____

Number: _____

Page _____ of _____

1	2	3	4	5	6	7	8	9	10	11	12	13	14	15	16	17	18
Pay Per. Ending Dates	Adjust. Stat. Value	Prod. Hours Stat.	Prod. Hours (2 × 3)	Nonprod. Factor	Nonprod. Hours (4 × 5) or ?	Total Pd. Hours (4 + 6)	Reg. Pay Rate	Reg. Pay Amount	Shift Diff. Amount	Call Pay Amount	Levels Adj.	O.T. Amount	Total Paid Amount	Accrual Factor	Total Monthly Budget	FICA (7%)	FICA Budget
4-14																	
4-28														0.14285		.07	
5-12																	
5-26														0.35714		.07	
6-9																	
6-23														0.50000		.07	
7-7																	
7-21														0.71428		.07	
8-4																	
8-18														0.92857		.07	
9-1																	
9-15																	
9-29														0.07142		.07	

F-3. Continued

Page_____of_____

	1	2	3	4	5	6	7	8	9	10	11	12	13	14	15	16	17	18
	Pay Per. Ending Dates	Adjust. Stat. Value	Prod. Hours Stat.	Prod. Hours (2 × 3)	Nonprod. Factor	Nonprod. Hours (4 × 5) or ?	Total Pd. Hours (4 + 6)	Reg. Pay Rate	Reg. Pay Amount	Shift Diff. Amount	Call Pay Amount	Levels Adj.	O.T. Amount	Total Paid Amount	Accrual Factor	Total Monthly Budget	FICA (7%)	FICA Budget
10-13																		
10-27															0.28571		.07	
11-10																		
11-24															0.42857		.07	
12-8																		
12-22															0.64286		.07	
1-5																		
1-19															0.85714		.07	
2-2																		
2-16															0.85714		.07	
3-2																		
3-16																		
3-30															0.07143		.07	
Totals															Total			

G. OPERATING EXPENSE SUMMARY: (Nonsalary)

Responsibility Center:

Name: _____

Number: _____

Page _____ of _____

Exp. Number	Exp. Name	Rate	Inflation Factor	Multi. Factor	Statistic	Apr.	May	June	July	Aug.	Sept.	Oct.	Nov.	Dec.	Jan.	Feb.	Mar.	Total
					Totals												

G-1. OPERATING EXPENSE BUDGET

Zero-Based—*Outside Personnel* 092

Responsibility Center:

Name: _____

Number: _____

Month	Category of Worker	Agency/Source	A Rate/Hr.	B Hours	Total A × B	Monthly Amount
						Total

G-2. OPERATING EXPENSE BUDGET

Zero-Based—Meetings and Travel 300

Responsibility Center:

Name: _____

Number: _____

Month	Traveler	Destination & Reason	A Regis. $	B Food & Lodging	Transportation	(A + B + C) Total	Monthly Total
						Total

G-3. OPERATING EXPENSE BUDGET

Zero-Based—*Committee Meetings* 302

Responsibility Center:

Name: _____

Number: _____

Month	Meeting	A No. Persons Attending	B Food Rate*	$(A + B = C)$ Food Total	D Supply Total	E Accom. Total	$(C + D + E)$ Meet. Total	Monthly Total
				Total				Total

*Food from Food Services (per person):

Coffee $0.50	Hot Lunches $4.52
Coffee & Donuts $0.85	Dinner $10.20
Cold Lunch $3.85	Stand-Up Events $7.25

G-4. OPERATING EXPENSE BUDGET

Zero-Based—Minor Equipment 355

Responsibility Center:

Name: _____

Number: _____

Month	Equipment	Vendor	Maintenance Agree. No. or Amt.*	Cost	Monthly Total
					Total
Total					

*If maintenance is not provided in the first-year warranty, enter the maintenance agreement cost anticipated for FY 198__–8__.

G-5. OPERATING EXPENSE BUDGET

Zero-Based—*Educational Expense* 460

Responsibility Center:

Name: _____

Number: _____

Month	Event	A No. Persons Attending	B Food Rate*	(A + B = C) Food Total	D Books & Supp.	E Accom. Total	(C + D + E) Meet Total	Monthly Total
			Total					Total

*Food from Food Services (per person):

Coffee $0.50	Hot Lunches $4.52
Coffee & Donuts $0.85	Dinner $10.20
Cold Lunches $3.85	Stand-Up Events $7.25

G-6. OPERATING EXPENSE BUDGET   Zero-Based—*Dues 689*

Responsibility Center:

Name: _____

Number: _____

Month	Member	Organization	Amount	Monthly Total
			Total	

G-7. OPERATING EXPENSE BUDGET

Zero-Based—*Subscriptions 690*

Responsibility Center:
Name: _____
Number: _____

Month	Publication	Where Filed	Amount	Month Total
			Total	

G-8. OPERATING EXPENSE BUDGET

Zero-Based—*Purchased Services—Corporation 750*

Responsibility Center:
Name: _____
Number: _____

Month	Service Purchased	From	Amount	Monthly Total
			Total	

G-9. OPERATING EXPENSE BUDGET

Zero-Based—Purchased Services—Individual 751

Responsibility Center:

Name: _____

Number: _____

Month	*Service Purchased*	*From*	*Amount*	*Monthly Total*
			Total	

G-10. OPERATING EXPENSE BUDGET

Zero-Based—*Equipment Rental 780*

Responsibility Center:

Name: _____

Number: _____

Month	Equipment Item	Rent From	Reason	Amount	Month Total
				Total	

G-11. OPERATING EXPENSE BUDGET

Zero-Based—*General*

Responsibility Center:

Name: _____

Number: _____

Natural Expense Account Number: _____

Natural Expense Account Name: _____

Month	Item or Event	Amount	Month Total
		Total	

Index

Italicized numerals indicate examples, figures, and forms

249